TIDEPOO

TIDEPOOLS
SOUTHERN CALIFORNIA

~~~~~~~~~~~~~~~~~~~~~~

AN ILLUSTRATED GUIDE TO 100 LOCATIONS
FROM POINT CONCEPTION TO MEXICO

LINDA E. TWAY, Ph.D.

To Jack —
I enjoyed meeting you
in Solana Beach —
With best wishes —
Linda Tway

CAPRA PRESS
SANTA BARBARA

Design by Cyndi Burt
Typography by Jim Cook

LIBRARY OF CONGRESS CATALOGING-IN-PUBLICATION DATA

Tway, Linda E.
  Tidepools of Southern California: an illustrated guide to
where they are / Linda Tway.
    p.   cm.
  Includes bibliographical references and index.
  ISBN 0-88496-322-5
  1. Tide pool ecology—California, Southern—Guide-
books.   2. Tide pools—California, Southern—Guide-
books.   3. Tide pool ecology—California, Southern—
Pictorial works.   4. Tide pools—California, Southern—
Pictorial works.   I. Title.
QH.105.C2T93   1991
574.5'2636—dc20   90-19864

Published by
CAPRA PRESS
Post Office Box 2068, Santa Barbara, CA 93120

Table of Contents

Foreword

Those of us who are fortunate enough to live near the coast, or to be able to visit it, cannot fail to be impressed by this timeless interface between mankind and nature. Even if we do no more than drive along it, the pressures of daily life are lightened by glimpses of vast, natural oceanic realm where air, water, rocks and living things maintain a balance that in many places is little affected by man.

Our pleasure and benefit are increased as we come closer to this boundary between ocean and land. Walking along the shore, we see at close hand the coves and headlands that have been sculpted by the ceaseless action of the waves, and the sandy beaches from which each tide erases our footprints but can only rearrange, not destroy, our trash.

In this book, Dr. Tway helps us to go one step further. To put on sneakers instead of town shoes, so as to be able to explore the actual, dynamic interaction between water, rocks and organisms. To time our visits in accordance with the rhythm of the tides, to stop more frequently and to look more closely. And with a deep sense of caring she shows us wonders that have been right in front of our noses, but unseen, all along.

A child who has been shown the beauty of a group of sand castle worms is unlikely to ever destroy such a delicate structure by a careless step. And to have really seen the delicate balance of the varied forms of life in a tidepool is the best (possibly the only) insurance against the unthinking removal of some essential members of that small community, and leaving them to die slowly in a bucket.

There is scarcely any other activity more satisfying and instructive than tidepooling. The more often we indulge in it, the more deeply we understand and appreciate the complex beauty of the natural world, and the less likely we are to damage it.

So take this opportunity to know it better, and enjoy it freely.

William R. Riedel, D.Sc.
Scripps Institution of Oceanography

This unique, generously illustrated guide to Southern California's tidepools describes nearly 100 intertidal sites from Santa Barbara to San Diego, and includes color photographs of the most common plants and animals. It serves the double purpose of making the living wonders of the intertidal zone accessible to a wider public, and of pointing out how to perpetuate this precious natural resource by treating it with respect.

Detailed locality maps introduce newcomers and tourists to the best places to view the biological communities of our intertidal zone, and suggest new localities for long-time residents to explore. School groups and classes will find this a valuable guide because of its discussion of intertidal ecology. Foreseeing the special needs of families with small children, Dr. Tway has provided information on available facilities, ease of access and the convenience of parking.

This informative book is recommended to anyone interested in exploring and learning about the intertidal environment of Southern California.

Donald W. Wilkie, Director
Scripps Aquarium-Museum

Purpose
of Book

This book was written with the explorer in mind. Several books already exist describing animal and plant life in Pacific Coast tidepools, but none tells you where to find these fascinating life forms. This book began as a result of my trying to find good tidepool localities for the oceanography field trips I was conducting. Though I had lived in Southern California for many years, I had yet to discover some of the best tidepools. Although "locals" know where they are, newcomers are usually in the dark. Now with this book, carefully compiled from research and countless field trips, I offer this easy guide to the tidepools of Southern California that shows you pathways, parking areas and tips on how to find the plant and animal life that abounds in tidepools. Through the introduction and descriptions of specific localities, you will also learn which organisms predominate and which are rare due to the particular ecological habitats of each area.

If you are like most people who visit tidepools for the first time, you will probably find yourself walking into the area oblivious to the richness of life thriving among the rocks. Yet by the time you leave, you will surely be tiptoeing your way out to avoid trampling the fragile plants and animals you discovered during your visit. There is much to enjoy and learn about tidepools, and I hope this book leads you through a rewarding adventure that sharpens your appreciation for life in Southern California's tidepools.

—L.T.

Acknowledgements

I would like to thank a number of colleagues and friends who generously donated their time for this project. Bill Riedel, Mia Tegner, and Bill Newman, all from Scripps Institution of Oceanography, Don Wilkie, Director of Scripps Aquarium-Museum, and Ed Spicer, also from Scripps Aquarium-Museum, reviewed the manuscript and offered suggestions that both improved and enhanced the book. I am especially grateful to Bill Riedel for accompanying me on some long and tedious field trips, and for writing the Foreword. Terry, Bill and Alexandra Gallant graciously put me up in their home while I did field work in Los Angeles and Ventura counties. My mother, Pat Tway, spent many foggy and rainy days with me in tidepools helping me to photograph some of the plants and shyer animals in this book. Others who helped in various ways include Annika Sanfilippo and Jesus Pineda (both at Scripps Institution of Oceanography), Julia Rennleitner, and Cindy Nelson. Thanks are also extended to my literary agent, Bill Gladstone (Waterside Productions), and publisher, Noel Young (Capra Press) for their interest in this book. Finally, I am most grateful to my husband, Bill Magdych, for helping with some of the field work and underwater photography, and for his encouragement during the course of this project.

—L.T.

Introduction

Tidepools occur wherever rocky land extends into the sea and the water level changes with the ebb and flow of the tides. At high tide, most of the area is submerged, and at low tide the rocks and many of the organisms attached to them are exposed while isolated pools of sea water harbor life that is more dependent on moisture. The causes of tides are explained in the Appendix, but for the purposes of this chapter it is only important to keep in mind that in Southern California, we experience roughly two high tides and two low tides each day. Predicted times and heights of these tides are listed in tide tables available for a nominal fee from watersport shops (such as surfing and diving stores) and institutions such as Sea World and Scripps Aquarium-Museum. The Appendix tells you how to interpret these tide tables.

Although sandy beaches are also subject to tidal fluctuations, there is less variety of life in the sand because most plants and animals have nothing to save them from being swept away. Sandy beaches are preferred by burrowing organisms such as worms, sand crabs and many types of clams. Thus, when we speak of tidepools, we are referring to places where organisms can firmly attach to rocks and crevices. The most varied life can be found in these areas, ranging from coral-like plants to exquisitely colored nudibranchs.

Several factors affect what life you might encounter in a tidepool area. Sunlight is one. During the early morning hours, you will see many more starfish, rock crabs, sea hares, giant keyhole limpets and other organisms that seek shelter from the midday sun. Similarly, on a rainy or overcast day you will usually see many more interesting tidepool creatures than on sunny days. Another factor is humidity. Santa Ana winds can dramatically drop the humidity, causing organisms to hide or even perish if tides are low. Seasonal variations are also important. Many types of algae flourish in the winter months but are nearly absent in the summer. Also we find that in the winter, more cobbles and rocks are exposed because the sand is swept away by winter storms. Many sandy beaches in the summer become cobbly in the

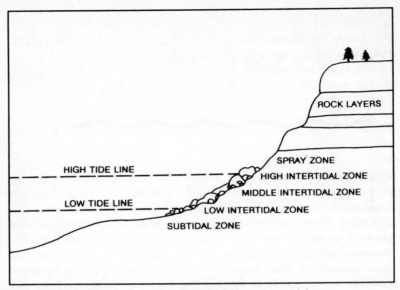

Figure 1. Cross-section of coastline showing different intertidal zones.

winter, making access more difficult. Yet winter is the best season to explore tidepools since daytime low tides are then the lowest (see Appendix), and the most is visible.

Physical factors are equally important since they determine which plants and animals can live in any particular area. A single intertidal area can be divided into several zones where environmental conditions differ (see Figure 1). The region nearest the cliffs or coastline is often called the *spray zone* because the only moisture hitting the rocks comes from splashing waves. The *intertidal zone* occurs below the spray zone and can be subdivided into *high, middle* and *low intertidal zones*. The high intertidal zone is exposed to air during any low tide, whereas the low intertidal zone is only exposed during the lowest low tides, while the middle intertidal zone is intermediate. High intertidal pools that are exposed are more subject to temperature changes because the iso-lated pools will warm quickly on sunny days and become cooler on chilly nights. Salinity (or salt content) can also vary due to evaporation and rainfall. The *subtidal zone* lies below the low intertidal zone and is always submerged. Many of the plants and animals living in the low intertidal zone also live in the subtidal zone.

Along with the physical zonations in tidepools we find biological ones as well. The spray zone is inhabited by organisms as well adapted to land as they are to sea, such as periwinkle snails and shore crabs. Because the high intertidal zone is exposed much of the time, organisms that live here must be well adapted to air exposure. They require ways of closing up and sealing in their moisture so that they don't dry out during periods of low tide. Here we commonly find mussels and barnacles. Both can seal themselves up with hard, moisture-resistant shells or plates to await the next high tide when they can again open up and feed on microscopic particles in the water. In the middle intertidal zone, we find organisms that can tolerate air but for shorter periods of time than those in the high intertidal. The low intertidal zone harbors those organisms that require moisture most of the time. Here we often encounter sponges, sea hares and starfish, none of which have any sort of adaptation to keep them from drying out. Fish are often found here, too.

Other factors also determine the type of life forms found in tidepools. The physical zonations discussed above are "universal" conditions that will affect biological zonations wherever tidepools exist. But local factors are also important. For example, local variations in coastline are extremely important in determining conditions that will favor certain life forms. We can see two examples of this on Southern California's coastline. An *embayment* is a place where the sea forms an inlet or small bay. Examples are the tidepools south of the Marine Room in La Jolla (San Diego County) and some of the large coves along the Palos Verdes peninsula (Los Angeles County). A *headland*, on the other hand, is a point of land or rock extending into the water. Examples include White Point (Los Angeles County), Alligator Head and Point Loma (both in San Diego County). An embayment has less wave activity and may be subject to more siltation than a headland. The greater the wave activity, the more oxygen aerates the water, and the more food particles sweep past hungry organisms. The tidepools just south of the Marine Room are protected from severe wave activity, and thus do not receive the well-aerated waters a headland receives. Therefore, we find fewer sea anemones at this locality, because they require well-oxygenated water. Protected embayments, however, favor other types of creatures as do areas with overhanging rocks. As long as good water flow exists, more delicate organisms can flourish without danger of being crushed by crashing waves. Sand castle worms are common in tidepools with overhanging rocks and plenty of sand. Headlands such as Alligator Head are subject to much greater wave action because they are rocky points jutting into the ocean (although thick offshore kelp beds can decrease this wave activity). In these areas, we find sea anemones flourishing in great numbers, not only because the waters here are so well aerated, but also because the increased water movement brings a greater abundance of food particles.

The nature of the rock composing tidepools also affects what you will find living there. Areas with abundant cobbles often have organisms able to scurry quickly to avoid being crushed by moving rocks. A good example is crabs (including hermit crabs), which abound in the tidepools at False Point (San Diego County) and along Palos Verdes (Los Angeles County). We also find limpets and acorn barnacles attached firmly to the cobbles because they can tolerate exposure to air and are fairly durable should they get hit by a wave-borne rock. Acorn barnacles are also better adapted to attaching to vertical faces and steeply sloping rocks than other organisms, and therefore they don't have to compete as vigorously for these "niches." Chitons and brittle stars hide under rocks and sea hares are well camouflaged among the cobbles. Therefore, we also find these organisms flourishing in the tidepools of False Point and other cobbly areas. Many tidepools in Southern California, however, are characterized by gently sloping, flat rock outcrops (or benches) which provide a stable place for attachment and tend to retain moisture for long periods of time. We find a different variety of organisms living in these tidepools. Especially abundant are leaf barnacles, sea anemones (assuming they are also in an area with lots of wave action) and mussels, all requiring a stable environment. We also find that tidepools with a variety of habitats (i.e. rock benches, boulders and shallow pools) have a greater variety of different life than tidepools that are predominantly of one habitat type (e.g. mainly boulders and cobbles).

Finally, the kind of rock in an area, for example sandstone or claystone, and the hardness of that rock has an effect on tidepool populations. Sandstones are coarse-grained rocks and provide a rough surface for attaching organisms, compared to a smooth rock, such as claystone, made up of tiny clay particles. Claystone is so fine-grained that most organisms find it too slippery to attach to effectively. You'll discover how slick they can be if you walk out on some wet claystones! Where claystone is dominant, fewer organisms can attach and they live mostly in tiny depressions and crevices. Examples of such areas are Gaviota State Beach (Santa Barbara County), Sunset Cliffs and Point Loma (both in San Diego County).

We also find that rocks vary in hardness. The rock that makes up the tidepools in many of the Laguna localities is very hard with a rough surface, making it ideal for attachment for many organisms. If the rock is too soft, as are many claystones, it erodes easily with wave activity and the organisms will be washed away. Fortunately, most rocks forming Southern California's coastline are hard enough to provide stable habitats for plants and animals. An interesting type of sandstone occurs at many of the localities described in this book, particularly in

La Jolla. This sandstone is hard enough to be stable in waves but soft enough to be scraped away by certain organisms. In this sandstone, we find thousands of oval depressions about an inch long. In each of these depressions is an animal called a chiton (pronounced "kite-un") (see Plate 34a & b) a type of mollusc with eight plates. The chiton scrapes the surface of the rock as it feeds on algae, creating a depression that matches its size and shape. Many of these depressions took 20 to 30 years of scraping to create—often by a succession of different chitons—and provide a protected habitat for them. Although this rock is an ideal environment for chitons, it is not stable enough for organisms such as barnacles, which permanently attach themselves, and they are conspicuously absent. This sandstone is gray to greenish but often has an unmistakable pink tinge due to a type of algae covering its surface. Heisler Park (Orange County), La Jolla Cove and North Bird Rock (both in San Diego County) are ideal places to see this fascinating relationship between geological and biological factors in tidepools.

Because of the various elements—both widespread and local—affecting what life can flourish in tidepools, you will want to be adventurous in your excursions. Tidepools can be full of discovery and surprise. The more you learn the more you will want to see. Don't hang back because you don't want to get your feet wet. Explore all the zones and regions to see firsthand the remarkable variety of life in tidepools and to glimpse the often fragile relationships between life and the physical world. But please, one caution—carefully replace any overturned rocks and leave the tidepools undisturbed. Laws prohibit the removal of *any* plants, animals, or even shells from many of our tidepools. They are yours to behold and protect.

Tidepool Safety and Conservation

Because tidepool rocks are generally wet and covered with slippery algae, be sure to walk slowly and carefully! Don't go barefoot because barnacles can cause painful cuts. Wear shoes with good tread and be sure you don't mind getting them wet. Wade through sandy areas with caution, shuffling your feet as you go, to frighten off any hidden stingrays. They can inflict painful wounds.

Visiting hours to tidepools should begin when the tide is receding, otherwise your retreat may be blocked off by the crashing waves of an incoming tide. (Refer to the Appendix for an explanation of tides and tide tables.) A rise of a scant foot in tide height can drastically alter the look (and safety) of an area. It is also best to visit a tidepool with a friend in case trouble should arise. If you are busy with your camera, your friend can warn you of approaching waves. If trouble occurs, two heads are better than one.

Equally important is taking pains to protect the plants and animals in tidepools. Many life forms have been living for decades. Growth rings of many sea palms indicate an age of seventy-five years or more, and sea anemones may live several hundred years if not disturbed! Tidepools were not "built overnight." It is up to you to preserve this natural habitat so that others after you may enjoy it, too. Tidepool creatures are easily damaged, and may die just from being handled. Brittle stars may lose an arm or two when you pick them up. Pulling other starfish from rocks tears their tube feet and arms and without a firm grip on rocks, they become easy prey for birds. If you pry loose a limpet, abalone or chiton and carelessly leave it upside down in the sun and air, you have left it to die, for it is impossible for it to right itself. Sea hares and nudibranchs are also damaged by air and should never be picked up or removed from the water. If you see a displaced tidepool creature, carefully return it to its natural habitat. Use utmost care and tread lightly when walking on the rocks to avoid crushing any life forms there. Although tiny barnacles on rocks can provide sure footing, their plates can be damaged beyond repair. If you cannot avoid the barnacles, walk as "lightly" as possible without twisting or grinding your feet sideways.

The rule for "tidepooling" is to *be careful*—for yourself and for the plants and animals living there. Many tidepool areas are protected by law and removing any plant or animal is illegal. If you want to take home a souvenir, bring your camera. Photographs are a much kinder and rewarding way to remember the array of life you'll see in tidepools.

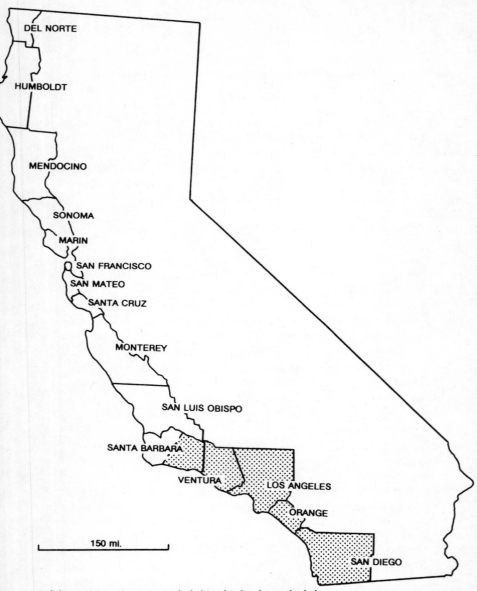

California Map. Counties included in this book are shaded.

DEL NORTE

HUMBOLDT

MENDOCINO

SONOMA

MARIN

SAN FRANCISCO

SAN MATEO

SANTA CRUZ

MONTEREY

SAN LUIS OBISPO

SANTA BARBARA

VENTURA

LOS ANGELES

ORANGE

SAN DIEGO

150 mi.

Places to go in Southern California

M ost plants and animals described in this book can be found at any of the tidepools included in this book. Keep in mind that local conditions will favor certain life forms. Also, some will be harder to see because they inhabit the low intertidal zone, which is submerged much of the time. The more abundant or unusual plants or animals you'll want to see are discussed in the following sections.

Tidepool locations are numbered consecutively from north to south for each county. A two-letter prefix corresponds to these numbers and indicates the county (SB for Santa Barbara County, VC for Ventura County, LA for Los Angeles County, OC for Orange County and SD for San Diego County). I have provided a map for each county as well as detailed maps for specific localities. For areas not along a major highway, I have included an intermediate map as well. All maps are oriented with NORTH at the top of the map as you read it. A distance scale is also provided. For some counties, notably Santa Barbara, Ventura and Los Angeles, directions in the text are generally referred to as "northwest" and "southeast" to avoid confusion that might result from the conflict of actual directions and street or highway directions. (For example, Hwy. 101 North runs east-west in many places.)

I have rated each locality on a scale of 1 to 5 (5 is the highest) based on accessibility, safety, and abundance of various life forms. The ratings are based on a low tide (generally negative). Ratings would be lower when the tide is higher. Only tidepools easily accessible to the public have been included. Many others exist, but have a difficult or private access, or are isolated and small. In winter months when beach sand is carried off by heavier waves, many more cobbly beaches become exposed. These areas are buried by sand in the summer and are not included in this book.

Although there is a fee to enter or park at most state or county beaches, these fees are often waived during the winter. Lifeguards are usually present only during summer months.

Locality descriptions only mention tidepool life in a broad sense to help you know what to look for. Detailed discussions of each plant and animal are presented in the last two chapters. My intention is to point out those life forms which are either most abundant or unique at a given tidepool area. You may want to keep your own log of discoveries at each tidepool you visit.

NOTE: COLLECTING ANY PLANT OR ANIMAL FROM TIDE-POOLS IS STRONGLY DISCOURAGED AND IS ILLEGAL AT MANY OF THEM. Many tidepools are part of a marine preserve, and collecting *anything* from these tidepools is illegal—including empty sea shells. Several other localities such as state, county or national parks, are protected and collecting most invertebrates is illegal as well. TO AVOID VIOLATION OF STATE AND FEDERAL LAWS AND TO HELP PRESERVE THE EXISTENCE OF CALIFORNIA'S TIDE-POOLS, DO NOT COLLECT FROM ANY OF THEM.

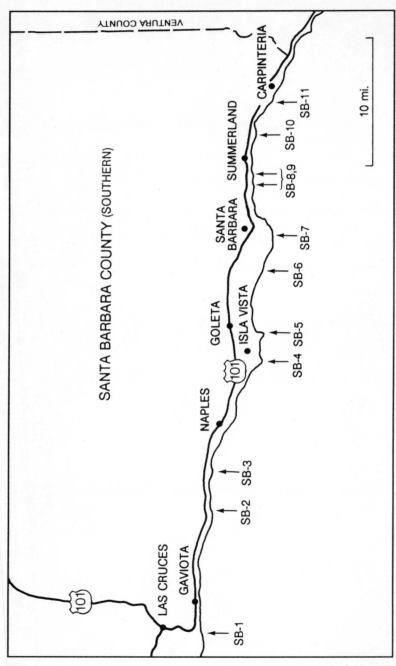

MAP 1

Santa Barbara County (Southern)

At Point Conception, just north of Gaviota State Beach, the ocean temperature drops considerably, causing a major ecological change, and supporting a different variety of marine plants and animals. Because of this, only the southern portion of Santa Barbara County (see Map 1) is included in this guide since it has tidepool life more consistent with the rest of Southern California. Be sure to visit the Sea Center on Stearns Wharf in Santa Barbara to see a variety of exhibits on the area's geology and marine life.

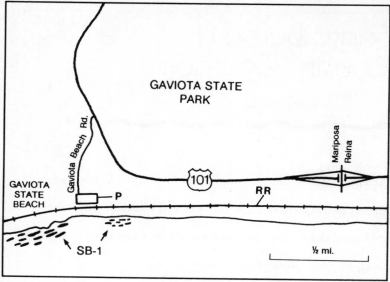

GAVIOTA STATE
PARK

Gaviota Beach Rd.

Mariposa Reina

GAVIOTA
STATE
BEACH

101

P

RR

SB-1

½ mi.

MAP 2

Locality SB-1
Gaviota State Beach (See Map 2)

These tidepools are best visited during a low negative tide. Although some tidepools exist southeast of the parking area, the northwestern rock benches are larger and contain the most interesting life. The steeply dipping rock layers are fine-grained, so most of the creatures are in the cracks and crevices. Be careful of waves if you explore rocks facing the surf.

RATING: 2

NATURE OF ROCKS: large, steeply dipping rock benches and boulders

ESPECIALLY ABUNDANT: California mussels, leaf barnacles, aggregating anemones, various limpets, sand castle worms, sea lettuce, feather boa kelp, surfgrass, chitons

PARKING/FEES: large parking lot with entry fee

ACCESS: easy walk from parking area

CAUTIONS: waves can hit rock benches with some force

FACILITIES: portable bathrooms, drinking fountains, picnic tables, telephones, lifeguard services

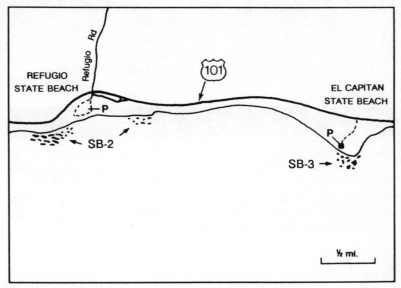

MAP 3

Locality SB-2
Refugio State Beach (See Map 3)

Tidepools here consist of cobbles, boulders and steeply dipping rock benches. Tidepools lie both northwest and southeast of the beach, although the most extensive rock benches occur to the northwest. Red sea urchins are particularly abundant among the cobbles, and purple olives and sand castle worms proliferate in the sandy areas.

 RATING: 3

NATURE OF ROCKS: cobbles, boulders and steeply dipping rock benches

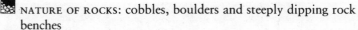 ESPECIALLY ABUNDANT: red sea urchins, purple sea urchins, ochre sea stars, sponges, purple olives, sand castle worms, giant green anemones, acorn barnacles, scaly tube snails, limpets, striped shore crabs, California mussels, leaf barnacles, volcano limpets, aggregating anemones, surfgrass, feather boa kelp, sea lettuce, coralline algae, volcano barnacles

OF SPECIAL INTEREST: abundant, colorful sponges and ochre sea stars in the low intertidal

PARKING/FEES: large parking lot with fee to enter park

ACCESS: easy walk from parking lot; tidepools are located both northwest and southeast of the beach, although the most extensive rock benches occur to the northwest

CAUTIONS: boulders and cobbles can be slippery

FACILITIES: public bathrooms, showers, drinking fountains, picnic tables, barbeque pits, telephones, camping, small store, lifeguard services

Locality SB-3
El Capitan State Beach (See Map 3)

This large beach park offers a variety of facilities including picnic areas, camping and a small store. A paved pathway leads from the west end of the parking lot to the beach. The bouldery tidepools are to the southeast. Aggregating anemones carpet many of the slippery rock surfaces, and many big ochre sea stars, giant green anemones, and huge California mussels also inhabit these pools.

RATING: 2

NATURE OF ROCKS: boulders and cobbles

ESPECIALLY ABUNDANT: aggregating anemones, leaf and acorn barnacles, limpets, sea lettuce, sand castle worms, ochre sea stars, giant green anemones, California mussels, feather boa kelp, sponge, surfgrass, pink encrusting coralline algae

PARKING/FEES: parking lots with fee to enter park

ACCESS: paved pathway leads from the west end of the parking lot to the beach; tidepools are to the southeast

CAUTIONS: rocks can be slippery

FACILITIES: public bathrooms, drinking fountains, showers, telephones, picnic tables, barbeque grills, camping, small store, lifeguard services

Locality SB-4
Isla Vista County Beach Park ("Coal Oil Pt.") (See Map 4)

Tidepools are extensive along the beach, especially to the northwest. This area is best visited during low tide.

Unfortunately, "Coal Oil Point," the northwest beach, is named for and tainted by oil which partially seeps naturally and is also due in part to offshore drilling. Some of the most interesting and largest scaly tube snails grow here. Farther northwest, aggregating anemones blanket many rocks.

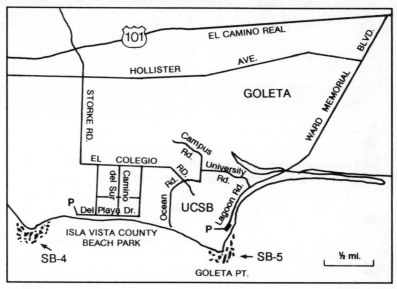

MAP 4

 RATING: 2

NATURE OF ROCKS: extensive, low rock benches

ESPECIALLY ABUNDANT: scaly tube snails, purple olives, surfgrass, giant green anemones, ochre sea stars, a variety of sponges, California mussels, leaf and acorn barnacles, California sea hares, wavy turbans, chestnut cowries, feather boa kelp, coralline algae, sargasso weed, sea lettuce, aggregating anemones

OF SPECIAL INTEREST: large scaly tube snails and purple olives

PARKING/FEES: small parking area at the west end of Del Playa Dr., and additional street parking nearby; no fees

ACCESS: a concrete stairway leads from the cliffs directly seaward of the parking area to the beach; tidepools are extensive along the beach, especially to the northwest

CAUTIONS: oil and sticky tar on beach

FACILITIES: none

Locality SB-5
Goleta Point (See Map 4)

To reach these tidepools, pay to park in lot #6 at the end of Lagoon Rd. on the campus of the University of California at Santa Barbara (UCSB). Big rock benches and boulders characterize these tidepools with a lot of oil on the nearby beach. Large ochre sea stars and scaly tube snails live in the low intertidal, and sandier areas harbor abundant purple olives.

RATING: 2

NATURE OF ROCKS: large rock benches and boulders

ESPECIALLY ABUNDANT: California mussels, leaf barnacles, ochre sea stars, giant green and aggregating anemones, acorn and volcano barnacles, scaly tube snails, purple olives, feather boa kelp, chitons, limpets, coralline algae

OF SPECIAL INTEREST: the low intertidal has some very large ochre sea stars and scaly tube snails, and the sandier areas harbor an abundance of purple olives.

PARKING/FEES: park in parking lot #6 at the end of Lagoon Rd. on the campus of the University of California, Santa Barbara; there is a nominal fee to enter the campus

ACCESS: at the northeast end of the parking lot there is a stairway leading to the beach; tidepools extend from the stairway to the point

CAUTIONS: oil on beach

FACILITIES: none

Locality SB-6
Arroyo Burro Beach County Park (See Map 5)

This pleasant beach park has tidepools both to the northwest and southeast, although the best ones are northwest. Visit this area during low, negative tide. Many purple olives and sand castle worms flourish in the sandier areas, while the low intertidal is inhabited by various colorful sponges, stalked tunicates and scaly tube snails.

RATING: 1½

NATURE OF ROCKS: low rock benches

ESPECIALLY ABUNDANT: purple olive snails, aggregating anemones, giant green anemones, scaly tube snails, sand castle worms, stalked tunicates, California mussels, leaf barnacles, variety of limpets, chitons, coralline algae, surfgrass, feather boa kelp

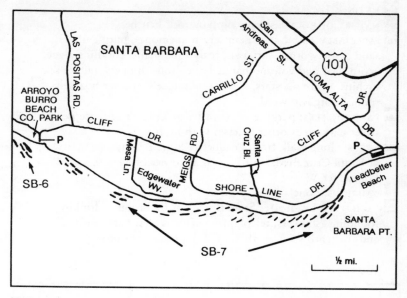

MAP 5

OF SPECIAL INTEREST: purple olives and sand castle worms in sandier areas; low intertidal is inhabited by an abundance of colorful sponges, stalked tunicates and scaly tube snails

PARKING/FEES: small parking lot; no fees

ACCESS: easy walk from parking area

CAUTIONS: none

FACILITIES: bathrooms, drinking fountains, showers, telephones, restaurant

Locality SB-7
Santa Barbara Point to Mesa Lane (See Map 5)

You can find access to these tidepools in three ways. One is from Leadbetter State Beach parking lot at the corner of Loma Alta Dr. and Shoreline Dr. where a fee is charged. The walk northwest to the tidepools is long. Another way is to descend a long stairway at the end of Santa Cruz Blvd., but the tidepools there are not as good. A third access is from the corner of Mesa Ln. and Edgewater Way where another long stairway leads to the beach. Tidepools are made of steeply dipping rock layers running along the shoreline. In general, you will see many giant green anemones, purple olives, sand castle worms and surfgrass; other life varies from spot to spot.

RATING: 1-2

NATURE OF ROCKS: steeply dipping rock benches

ESPECIALLY ABUNDANT: giant green anemones, purple olives, sand castle worms, surfgrass, scaly tube snails, coralline algae, acorn, leaf and volcano barnacles, chitons, limpets, purple sea urchins, ochre sea stars, California mussels, feather boa kelp, sponge, sargasso weed

PARKING/FEES: parking lot with fee at Leadbetter State Beach; street parking at other accesses with no fee

ACCESS: long walk from Leadbetter State Beach; long stairways at Santa Cruz Blvd.; third access at corner of Mesa Ln. and Edgewater Way

CAUTIONS: none

FACILITIES: Leadbetter State Beach has bathrooms, drinking fountains, showers, telephones, picnic tables, barbeque grills and lifeguard services; there is also a restaurant nearby

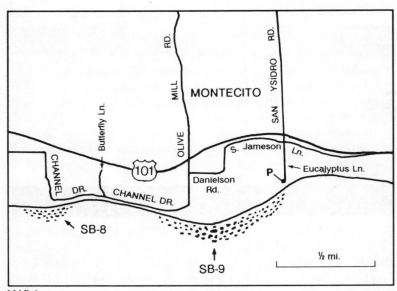

MAP 6

Locality SB-8
Butterfly Lane (See Map 6)

These cobbly, bouldery tidepools extend northwest of the beach access at the corner of Butterfly Ln. and Channel Dr. The large intermittent sandy areas harbor abundant purple olive snails and sand castle worms while sargasso weed and feather boa kelp fill many of the pools.

RATING: 1½

NATURE OF ROCKS: cobbles and boulders

ESPECIALLY ABUNDANT: surfgrass, aggregating anemones, pink encrusting coralline algae, purple olives, sand castle worms, limpets, giant green anemones, acorn barnacles, sargasso weed, sea lettuce, feather boa kelp, coralline algae, scaly tube snails

PARKING/FEES: street parking along Channel Dr.; no fees

ACCESS: long but easy walk from the corner of Butterfly Ln. and Channel Dr.

CAUTIONS: slippery cobbles

FACILITIES: none

Locality SB-9
Eucalyptus Lane to Channel Dr. (See Map 6)

The south end of San Ysidro Rd. off Hwy. 101 becomes Eucalyptus Lane, leading to a small parking area with easy access to cobbly tidepools. You may also reach these pools by parking along Channel Dr. near the intersection of Olive Mill Rd. Other cobbly tidepools occur farther southeast, although they are not as extensive. Be sure the tides are negative when you visit these pools. Large, colorful giant green anemones and abundant aggregating anemones inhabit these pools.

RATING: 2

NATURE OF ROCKS: cobbles and boulders

ESPECIALLY ABUNDANT: aggregating and giant green anemones, surfgrass, scaly tube snails, sand castle worms, California sea hares, purple olives, sargasso weed, tegulas, periwinkles, hermit crabs, limpets, acorn barnacles, ochre sea stars, coralline red algae, feather boa kelp, sea lettuce, rock crabs

PARKING/FEES: small parking lot at the end of Eucalyptus Ln.; street parking along Channel Dr.; no fees

ACCESS: short walk from Eucalyptus Ln. or Channel Dr.

CAUTIONS: cobbles are slippery

FACILITIES: none

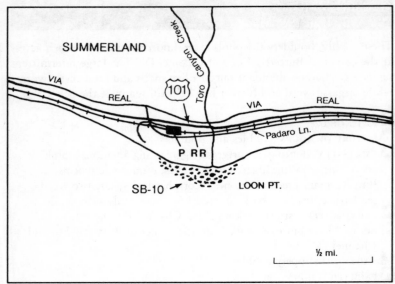

MAP 7

Locality SB-10
Loon Point (See Map 7)

Extensive, bouldery tidepools at Loon Point are rich with aggregating anemones and sponges. If you stand in the low intertidal and look southeast at the boulders, you will see rocks covered with bright orange splashes, some are ochre sea stars, but most are velvety red sponges. Various crabs are also present, including rock crabs partially burrowed in the sand at the edges of the rocks.

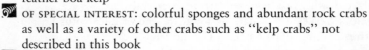

RATING: 2

NATURE OF ROCKS: boulders and cobbles

ESPECIALLY ABUNDANT: aggregating anemones, sponges, variety of crabs, ochre sea stars, California mussels, scaly tube snails, leaf, acorn and volcano barnacles, limpets, chitons, surfgrass, feather boa kelp

OF SPECIAL INTEREST: colorful sponges and abundant rock crabs as well as a variety of other crabs such as "kelp crabs" not described in this book

PARKING/FEES: large parking lot at the northwest end of Padaro Ln.

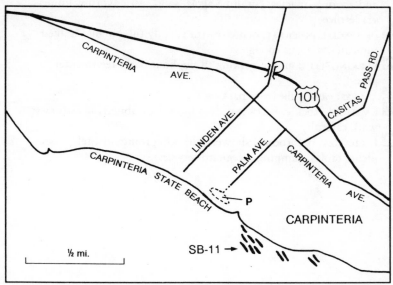

MAP 8

ACCESS: long pathway leads from northwest end of parking lot, underneath a bridge and finally ends at beach

CAUTIONS: rocks can be slippery

FACILITIES: portable bathrooms along path

Locality SB-11
Carpinteria State Beach (See Map 8)

The most direct route to Carpinteria State Beach is via Casitas Pass Rd. exit off of Hwy. 101. At the entrance at the end of Palm Ave. you must pay a fee to enter. Park at the southeast end and avoid a long walk to the tidepools by following the road bearing right just as you leave the park. Rock benches, although not extensive, are rich with life, especially aggregating anemones and large, colorful giant green anemones. Sponges, ochre sea stars, scaly tube snails and stalked tunicates live in this area surrounded by a pleasant beach park.

RATING: 3½

NATURE OF ROCKS: large rock benches

ESPECIALLY ABUNDANT: sponges, giant green and aggregating anemones, surfgrass, feather boa kelp, ochre sea stars, stalked tunicates, scaly tube snails, California mussels, leaf, volcano and acorn barnacles, coralline algae, sand castle worms, limpets, sea lettuce

OF SPECIAL INTEREST: ochre sea stars, scaly tube snails, stalked tunicates, various sponges

PARKING/FEES: ample parking throughout park; fee to enter park

ACCESS: easy walk from parking lot

CAUTIONS: rock crevices are often hidden by abundant surfgrass; walk carefully

FACILITIES: bathrooms, showers, drinking fountains, telephones, picnic tables, camping, lifeguard services.

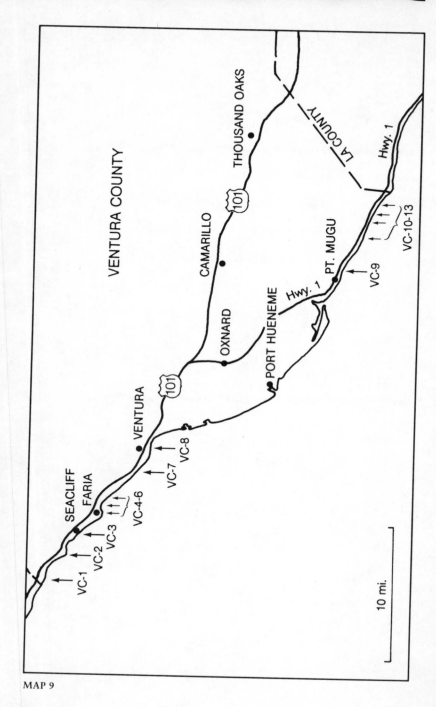

MAP 9

Ventura County

Most of the Ventura County coastline (see Map 9) is made up of long stretches of sandy beaches. Although there are more tidepools in the northern part of the county, the few rock benches that occur in the southern part harbor much more interesting and diverse life.

NORTHERN VENTURA COUNTY

[Tidepools in northern Ventura County (see Map 9) are composed mainly of boulders and cobbles, making them more barren and less interesting than their counterparts in the south county. Still, they are worth a visit.]

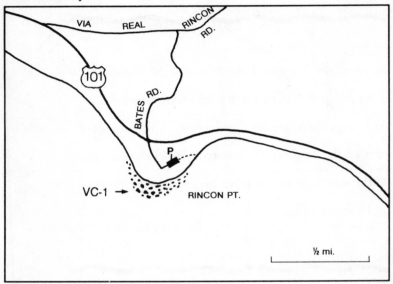

MAP 10

Locality VC-1
Rincon Point (See Map 10)

This is the southernmost end of Carpinteria State Beach. At the eastern end of the parking lot you will find a chainlink fence with a gate opening upon a long, dirt path leading to the east side of Rincon Point. Extensive tidepools are to the west. If you continue in this direction, you'll find larger rocks harboring more diverse life. Aggregating anemones cover many of the rocks. Don't step on them or you will kill them. Although diversity at Rincon Point is low, the life present is abundant.

 RATING: 1½

NATURE OF ROCKS: cobbles and boulders

ESPECIALLY ABUNDANT: giant green anemones, acorn barnacles,

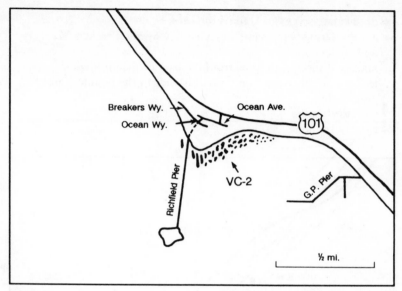

MAP 11

tegula snails, hermit crabs, purple olives, limpets, feather boa kelp, surfgrass, California mussels, ochre sea stars, sand castle worms, scaly tube snails

 PARKING/FEES: large parking lot; no fee

ACCESS: long pathway from parking lot

CAUTIONS: cobbles are slippery

FACILITIES: none

Locality VC-2
Mussel Shoals (See Map 11)

A sign on Highway 101 indicates the turnoff for Mussel Shoals, a name derived from the area's abundant California mussels, but mussels are not alone here. Aggregating anemones carpet many rocks in a speckled white, while stalked tunicates droop from rocks like wilted flower buds.

RATING: 3

NATURE OF ROCKS: mainly large boulders and cobbles

ESPECIALLY ABUNDANT: California mussels, giant green anemones, aggregating anemones, leaf barnacles, sponge, stalked tunicates, feather boa kelp, ochre sea stars, acorn barnacles, striped shore crabs, purple olives, limpets, scaly tube snails, sand castle worms

OF SPECIAL INTEREST: stalked tunicates

PARKING/FEES: on street along Ocean Way and Breakers Way; no fee

ACCESS: a short path leads from the base of the pier (which leads to an oil refinery on a small island) to the bouldery area just south

CAUTIONS: none

FACILITIES: none

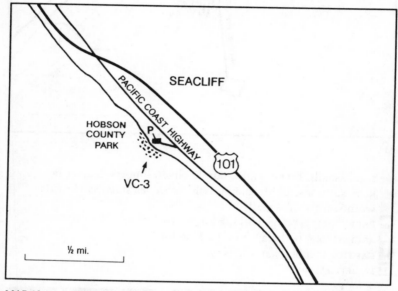

MAP 12

Locality VC-3
Hobson County Park (See Map 12)

Cobbly tidepools at this small park off Pacific Coast Highway harbor such interesting life as large, bright giant green anemones and budlike stalked tunicates.

RATING: 1½

NATURE OF ROCKS: cobbles and boulders

ESPECIALLY ABUNDANT: giant green anemones, coralline algae, acorn barnacles, purple olives, striped shore crabs, sea lettuce, scaly tube snails, ochre sea stars, stalked tunicates, feather boa kelp, surfgrass

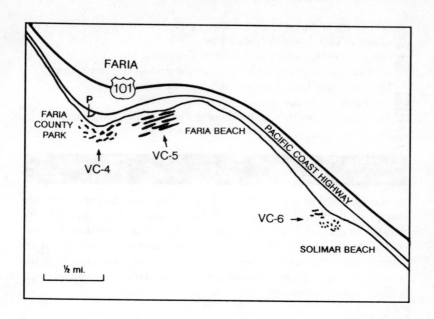

OF SPECIAL INTEREST: stalked tunicates in the low intertidal

PARKING/FEES: parking lot; there is a fee to camp

ACCESS: a short stairway at the north end of parking lot leads to the cobbly tidepools

CAUTIONS: rocks are slippery

FACILITIES: picnic tables, barbecue grills, portable bathrooms, camping

Locality VC-4
Faria County Park (See Map 13)

Cobbly tidepools in this small county park off Pacific Coast Highway maintain a variety of life including California mussels, anemones, surfgrass and feather boa kelp. Coralline red algae and pink encrusting coralline algae bathe many rocks in pink. As in any cobbly tidepools, the rocks here can be very slippery.

RATING: 2

NATURE OF ROCKS: cobbles and boulders

ESPECIALLY ABUNDANT: California mussels, leaf barnacles, giant green and aggregating anemones, sand castle worms, ochre sea stars, surfgrass, feather boa kelp, striped shore crabs, limpets, acorn barnacles, coralline red algae, pink encrusting coralline algae, volcano barnacles, sea lettuce

PARKING/FEES: parking lot; there is a camping fee

ACCESS: a small stairway leads from the middle of the parking lot, over some large boulders and into the tidepools

CAUTIONS: rocks are slippery

FACILITIES: picnic tables, barbecue grills, portable bathrooms, camping

Locality VC-5
Faria Beach (See Map 13)

At the west end of the small cove just east of Faria County Park, are extensive tidepools consisting of cobbles and steeply dipping rock layers parallel to the beach in the low intertidal. This awkward rock grade covered in abundant surfgrass is difficult to traverse. However, it is an interesting mixture of environments to explore. Although the diversity is low, the existing life forms tend to be abundant, with sponges and stalked tunicates profuse.

RATING: 2

NATURE OF ROCKS: steeply dipping rock layers

ESPECIALLY ABUNDANT: surfgrass, feather boa kelp, giant green anemones, sand castle worms, purple olives, sponges, stalked tunicates, scaly tube snails, coralline red algae, sea lettuce

OF SPECIAL INTEREST: sponges and stalked tunicates are very common

PARKING/FEES: parking along Pacific Coast Highway; no fees

ACCESS: short walk from Pacific Coast Highway

CAUTIONS: difficult to traverse due to steeply dipping rocks and crevices hidden by surfgrass

FACILITIES: none

Locality VC-6
Solimar Beach (See Map 13)

Three small tidepool areas appear along Solimar Beach. The central and southern ones are cobbly (with a rating of "1") and have a low diversity of life. In the low intertidal, rocks are smothered in surfgrass; giant green anemones and purple olive snails abound. Farther north, a small rock bench extends away from the beach. Rated a "2," this is the best area to visit if you have a very low tide. Colorful sponges literally cover the wetter rock surfaces.

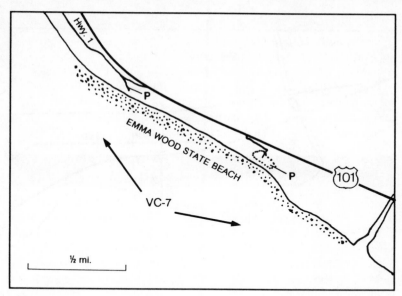

MAP 14

■ RATING: 1-2
■ NATURE OF ROCKS: cobbles and some rock benches
■ ESPECIALLY ABUNDANT: giant green and aggregating anemones, purple olives, feather boa kelp, small acorn barnacles, sea lettuce, chitons, limpets, sponges, surfgrass, California mussels, ochre sea stars
■ OF SPECIAL INTEREST: ochre sea stars and sponges
■ PARKING/FEES: parking along Pacific Coast Highway
■ ACCESS: access is from the north or south of the private housing development along the beach
■ CAUTIONS: none
■ FACILITIES: none

Locality VC-7
Emma Wood State Beach (See Map 14)

In order to visit these cobbly and sandy tidepools, you will need a low, negative tide. Although the pools are extensive, life forms are sparse and not very diverse. However, you will see brilliant giant green anemones among the cobbles, and colorful sponges in the low intertidal. The northwest end of the beach has more easily accessible pools, and there is no fee to enter here. If you enter the beach park to the southeast, there is a fee and a long walk to the beach.

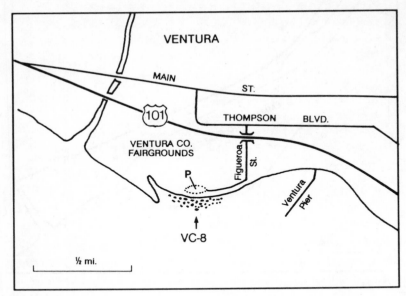

MAP 15

RATING: 1½

NATURE OF ROCKS: cobbles

ESPECIALLY ABUNDANT: giant green anemones, sand castle worms, purple olives, acorn barnacles, sponges, various limpets, feather boa kelp, surfgrass, volcano barnacles, pink encrusting coralline algae

OF SPECIAL INTEREST: colorful sponges in the low intertidal

PARKING/FEES: large lots; no fee at northwest end of beach

ACCESS: short walk from parking area (at north end of beach)

CAUTIONS: cobbles are slippery

FACILITIES: portable bathrooms, telephones, camping

Locality VC-8
Ventura County Fairgrounds (See Map 15)

Enter the fairgrounds parking lot at the south end of Figueroa St. and park at the west end of the lot. Although the cobbly tidepools are vast, diversity and abundance are low. Plants and animals typical of cobbly areas are common, and some amazingly large giant green anemones appear in the wetter areas.

■ RATING: 1

■ NATURE OF ROCKS: cobbles

■ PRESENT BUT NOT ABUNDANT: tegulas, hermit crabs, limpets, acorn barnacles, giant green anemones, sea lettuce, feather boa kelp, surfgrass

■ PARKING/FEES: large parking lot; no fees

■ ACCESS: short walk from parking lot

■ CAUTIONS: cobbles are slippery

■ FACILITIES: bathrooms, showers, drinking fountains and lifeguard services are available at the east end of the parking lot

SOUTHERN VENTURA COUNTY

[*The sandy beaches and lagoons between Ventura and Point Mugu (see Map 9) do not provide suitable tidepool habitats. Some small tidepool areas consisting of large boulders and rock benches harboring tidepool life appear in the southern portion of Ventura County. They may be reached via frequent pulloffs along Pacific Coast Highway. Some of the more well-defined localities are described below.*]

Locality VC-9
Thornhill Broome State Beach (La Jolla Canyon) (See Map 16)

If you simply want to visit tidepools and avoid state beach fees, park along Pacific Coast Highway. Although scattered boulders abound at the northwest end of the beach, the better tidepools are associated with large rock benches at the southeast end. If you climb down to the lower rocks, you may see some interesting ochre sea stars, but be careful of the strong surf.

■ RATING: 2

■ NATURE OF ROCKS: large rock benches

■ ESPECIALLY ABUNDANT: sea lettuce, periwinkles, acorn barnacles, California mussels, feather boa kelp, ochre sea stars

■ PARKING/FEES: parking along Pacific Coast Highway for free, or within the park for a fee

■ ACCESS: short walk from Pacific Coast Highway; path is steep

■ CAUTIONS: surf is strong on outer rock faces

■ FACILITIES: camping, picnic tables, restrooms, showers, drinking fountains, lifeguard services.

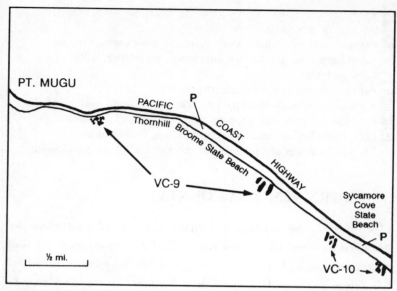

PT. MUGU

PACIFIC

Thornhill Broome State Beach

COAST

HIGHWAY

P

VC-9

Sycamore
Cove
State
Beach

P

VC-10 →

½ mi.

MAP 16

Locality VC-10
Sycamore Cove State Beach (See Map 16)

Scattered boulders and rock benches at both ends of this beach harbor tidepool life. Ochre sea stars cling to rock faces in the surf zone. Tidepools are not extensive, and it is somewhat difficult to climb over some of the larger rocks.

RATING: 1

NATURE OF ROCKS: boulders and rock benches

ESPECIALLY ABUNDANT: sand castle worms, giant green anemones, aggregating anemones, California mussels, leaf barnacles, ochre sea stars, acorn barnacles, feather boa kelp, coralline algae, sea lettuce, limpets, chitons

PARKING/FEES: park either along Pacific Coast Highway or within the park itself for a fee

ACCESS: short walk from Pacific Coast Highway

CAUTIONS: beware of strong surf at seaward edge of rocks

FACILITIES: camping, picnic tables, portable bathrooms, lifeguard services

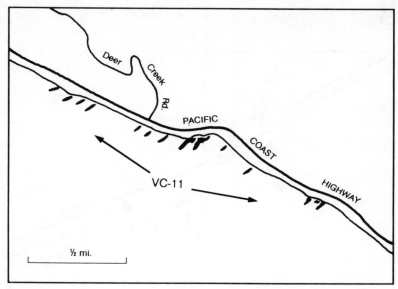

MAP 17

Locality VC-11
Sycamore Canyon to Yerba Buena (See Map 17)

Various rock benches along Pacific Coast Highway between Sycamore Canyon and Yerba Buena Rd. are the home to limited, but impressive tidepool life. The rating varies with the different tidepools here, but the better ones are found at the northern end. Abundant purple, orange, red and brown ochre sea stars paint a striking scene, touched by the colorful array of sponges nearby and given texture by California mussels, leaf barnacles and aggregating anemones.

RATING: 2-3

NATURE OF ROCKS: rock benches

ESPECIALLY ABUNDANT: California mussels, ochre sea stars, leaf barnacles, aggregating anemones, volcano barnacles, sponges, striped shore crabs, giant owl limpets, chitons, coralline red algae, feather boa kelp, surfgrass

OF SPECIAL INTEREST: colorful ochre sea stars and sponges

PARKING/FEES: parking along Pacific Coast Highway; no fees

ACCESS: three coastal accesses occur along this stretch and are marked by signs, two of which have concrete steps; one access is just west of Deer Creek Rd.

CAUTIONS: none
FACILITIES: none

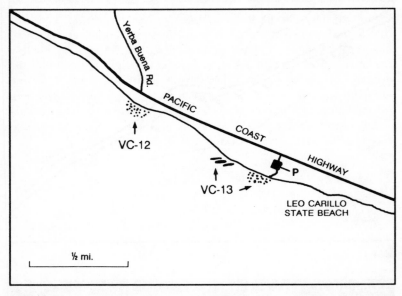

MAP 18

Locality VC-12
Yerba Buena (See Map 18)

Interesting sand castle worms and scaly tube snails flourish in this small cobbly point just south of Yerba Buena Rd. Be careful walking around the slippery cobbles.

RATING: 2
NATURE OF ROCKS: cobbles
ESPECIALLY ABUNDANT: sand castle worms, scaly tube snails, sargasso weed, California sea hares, aggregating anemones, giant green anemones, ochre sea stars, feather boa kelp, surfgrass, purple olives, acorn barnacles, volcano limpets
PARKING/FEES: parking along Pacific Coast Highway; no fees
ACCESS: short pathway from Pacific Coast Highway
CAUTIONS: cobbles are slippery
FACILITIES: none

Locality VC-13
Leo Carrillo State Beach/Ventura Co (See Map 18)

Interesting tidepools are located at the northwestern end of Leo Carrillo State Beach, which extends from Ventura County into northern Los Angeles County. It is easy to miss the parking lot entrance because the beach sign is not posted on Pacific Coast Highway but adjoins the driveway on the west side of the highway in the 40000 block. A long dirt path leads from the southeast end of the lot to the beach. Two tidepool areas appear along the beach. The southern one is quite cobbly and bouldery (rating a "1") while the northern area has some good rock benches (rating a "2"). Be careful of slippery rocks.

RATING: 1-2

NATURE OF ROCKS: cobbles and rock benches

ESPECIALLY ABUNDANT: giant green anemones, aggregating anemones, sand castle worms, limpets, feather boa kelp, California mussels, acorn barnacles, chitons, coralline red algae, surfgrass, ochre sea stars, leaf barnacles, scaly tube snails

OF SPECIAL INTEREST: sponges in the low intertidal

PARKING/FEES: large parking lot; no fees

ACCESS: long dirt pathway at southeast end of lot

CAUTIONS: cobbly area is slippery

FACILITIES: none

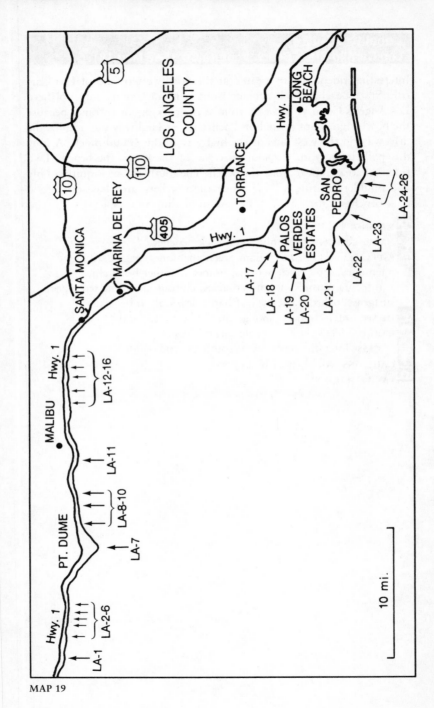

MAP 19

Los Angeles County

In spite of Los Angeles' high population, there are many tidepools that are relatively unspoiled in this busy area. Although the central part of the county (see Map 19) is typified by long, sandy beaches, the northern and southern parts of the county provide the visitor with some very impressive tidepools.

NORTHERN LOS ANGELES COUNTY

[Northern Los Angeles County (see Map 19) is well known for its sweeping beaches. In these sandy areas the occasional tidepools that do occur are generally small and made up of large boulders and cobbles. There are, however, a few extensive and rewarding tidepools in this area, notably from Paradise Cove to Dume Cove.]

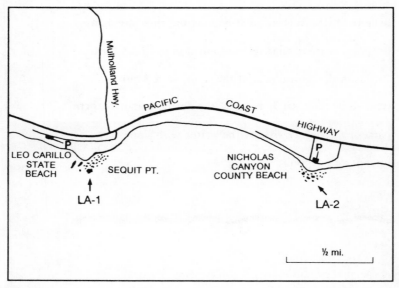

MAP 20

Locality LA-1
Leo Carrillo State Beach/Los Angeles Co. (See Map 20)

To visit this area, either park gratis along Pacific Coast Highway, or pay to enter the state beach on the west side of the highway. The beach parking lot however, is northwest of Sequit Point which lacks good tidepools, and is quite a distance away from the southeast end where the best tidepools are. Most of the smaller boulders and cobbles in these pools are covered with algae and are very slippery. Be sure to look at the larger rock benches which harbor a greater variety of interesting plants and animals.

RATING: 4

NATURE OF ROCKS: cobbles, boulders and rock benches

ESPECIALLY ABUNDANT: hermit crabs, tegulas, sea hares, sand castle worms, scaly tube snails, sponges, chitons, California mussels, leaf barnacles, anemones (both giant green and aggregating), purple and red sea urchins, ochre sea stars, feather boa kelp, surfgrass, coralline red algae, sargasso weed, sea lettuce, acorn barnacles, purple olive, striped shore crabs, limpets

OF SPECIAL INTEREST: sponges and thousands of chitons burrowed in soft sandstone

PARKING/FEES: park for free along Pacific Coast Highway; there is a fee to enter the park

ACCESS: easy walk from Pacific Coast Highway or parking lot

CAUTIONS: cobbles are very slippery

FACILITIES: public restrooms, lifeguard services, camping, store, telephones and other facilities.

Locality LA-2
Nicholas Canyon County Beach (See Map 20)

As with most of the northern L.A. localities, slippery boulders and cobbles make up the tidepools here. The most interesting aspect of Nicholas Canyon County Beach tidepools is the abundant red, yellow and white sponges coating submerged rocks in the low intertidal zone.

RATING: 2

NATURE OF ROCKS: cobbles and boulders

ESPECIALLY ABUNDANT: California mussels, sand castle worms, aggregating anemones, sponges, acorn and volcano barnacles, large chitons, ochre sea stars, surfgrass, sargasso weed, feather boa kelp, sea hares, giant green anemones, scaly tube snails

OF SPECIAL INTEREST: variety of colorful sponges

PARKING/FEES: large parking lots; no fees

ACCESS: short steep pathway from lower parking lot

CAUTIONS: rocks are very slippery

FACILITIES: telephone and portable bathrooms (at upper parking lot), lifeguard services on beach northwest of tidepools.

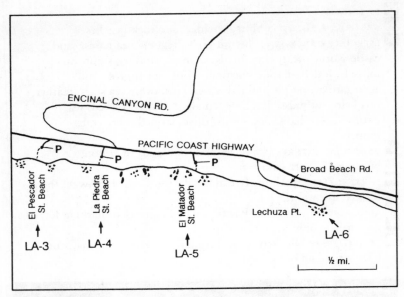

MAP 21

Locality LA-3
El Pescador State Beach (See Map 21)

A long, dirt pathway leads to a sandy cove with bouldery tidepools at both ends of the beach; the southeastern pools are the best. Wetter areas harbor plentiful ochre sea stars and sponges. Some large chitons are attached to drier rocks, hidden behind a carpeting of algae.

RATING: 2

NATURE OF ROCKS: cobbles and boulders

ESPECIALLY ABUNDANT: California mussels, sponges, chitons, aggregating anemones, sand castle worms, surfgrass, feather boa kelp, ochre sea stars, giant green anemones, giant owl limpets, coralline red algae, purple olives, California sea hares, leaf and acorn barnacles

OF SPECIAL INTEREST: large chitons, sponges, ochre sea stars

PARKING/FEES: small parking lot with self-registration fee; free parking along Pacific Coast Highway

ACCESS: a long dirt pathway leads to the cove from the parking lot

CAUTIONS: rocks are slippery

FACILITIES: portable bathrooms, telephone.

Locality LA-4
La Piedra State Beach (See Map 21)

A long dirt path leads from the northwest corner of the parking lot to a cobbly beach. Be careful walking on the cobbles as many are covered with algae and are very slippery. Tidepools are extensive, but lack diversity and abundance. Some high rocks are present in the southeast. If the tide is low, climb out on these pink, coralline algae-covered rocks to see a wider variety of life.

RATING: 2

NATURE OF ROCKS: cobbles and boulders

ESPECIALLY ABUNDANT: scaly tube snails, purple olives, anemones, various limpets, feather boa kelp, surfgrass, sea lettuce, coralline algae, sargasso weed, sand castle worms, California mussels, leaf barnacles, chitons, giant owl limpets

PARKING/FEES: small parking lot with self-registration fee

ACCESS: a long, dirt pathway leads from the northwest corner of the parking lot behind portable bathrooms down to the cobbly beach

CAUTIONS: rocks are very slippery

FACILITIES: picnic tables, portable bathrooms, telephone.

Locality LA-5
El Matador State Beach (See Map 21)

Scattered rock boulders and some very high "monoliths" compose this area. Diversity and richness are impressive. Abundant volcano limpets attached to upper rock surfaces are especially striking. Many boulders are covered with spectacular sand castle worm clusters. Cobbly pools harboring California sea hares, scaly tube snails and sargasso weed are located in the northwest, and purple olives are common in sandy areas.

RATING: 4

NATURE OF ROCKS: boulders, "monoliths" and cobbly pools

ESPECIALLY ABUNDANT: California mussels, leaf barnacles, aggregating anemones, sand castle worms, giant green anemones, feather boa kelp, coralline algae, chitons, volcano limpets, California sea hares, scaly tube snails, sargasso weed, purple olives

OF SPECIAL INTEREST: abundant volcano limpets on top of rocks

PARKING/FEES: small parking lot with self-pay fee or park for free along Pacific Coast Highway

ACCESS: long dirt path and stairway

CAUTIONS: cobbly area is slippery

FACILITIES: portable bathrooms at parking lot; lifeguard services.

Locality LA-6
Lechuza Point (See Map 21)

A gated public access in the 31300 block of Broad Beach Rd. leads to a sandy beach. Tidepools lie at the northwest point and consist of boulders and cobbles which can be difficult to traverse. Feather boa kelp, California mussels, rockweed, leaf barnacles and scaly tube snails are particularly numerous, and ochre sea stars cling to the sides and undersides of rocks.

RATING: 3

NATURE OF ROCKS: boulders and cobbles

ESPECIALLY ABUNDANT: feather boa kelp, California mussels, rockweed, leaf barnacles, scaly tube snails, ochre sea stars, purple olives, giant green anemones, chitons, various limpets

PARKING/FEES: free along Broad Beach Rd.

ACCESS: gated public access in 31300 block of Broad Beach Rd.; long but easy walk to tidepools at point northwest of this access

CAUTIONS: rocks are difficult to get around and are slippery

FACILITIES: lifeguard services.

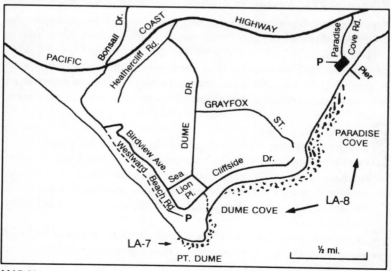

MAP 22

Locality LA-7
Point Dume (See Map 22)

When visiting Point Dume, park at the southeastern end of the parking lot along Westward Beach Rd. This tidepool area is rich with abundant life clinging to steep rocks. California mussels and leaf barnacles are particularly common. The rocks are volcanic and much harder than the softer rock layers visible in the cliffs northwest of the point. Volcanic activity created steep cliff faces, so be careful as the tidepools are somewhat difficult to traverse.

RATING: 3½

NATURE OF ROCKS: large rock benches, boulders and "monoliths"

ESPECIALLY ABUNDANT: California mussels, leaf barnacles, sea stars, aggregating anemones, giant green anemones, sponges, sand castle worms, chitons, giant owl limpets, acorn barnacles

OF SPECIAL INTEREST: abundant velvaty red sponges and ochre sea stars

PARKING/FEES: large parking lot along Westward Beach Rd.; no fees

ACCESS: short walk from southeast end of parking lot

CAUTIONS: rock faces are very steep and difficult to climb; also beware of strong surf hitting the seaward rockfaces

FACILITIES: lifeguard services all along beach, restrooms, showers, drinking fountains

Locality LA-8
Paradise Cove to Dume Cove (See Map 22)

Exploring from Paradise Cove to Dume Cove is the best tidepool tour in northern L.A. County. The walk takes an hour or two, depending on how much time you spend at each pool. If you walk the entire distance, be sure to allow plenty of low-tide time. The beach is also a great place for a picnic. Tidepools are extensive, easily accessible and full of diverse life, especially just east of Dume Cove. Because diversity and abundance change along the way, the rating varies from 2-4. Long expanses of bench-like rocks extend out from the beach, providing ideal attachment surfaces for a multitude of tidepool life. Spectacular sand castle worms cover many rocks—some of the sandy masses resemble rocks themselves.

The best access is from Paradise Cove. Turn seaward onto Paradise Cove Rd. from Pacific Coast Highway at the traffic light and drive to the end. Paying to park in the lot is well worth the fee. Alternatively, a hole in the chainlink fence just west of Dume Dr. leads to a long steep path to Dume Cove.

RATING: 2-4

NATURE OF ROCKS: large rock benches, boulders and cobbles

ESPECIALLY ABUNDANT: striped shore crabs, aggregating and giant green anemones, California mussels, leaf barnacles, sand castle worms, ochre sea stars, volcano barnacles, ochre sea stars, feather boa kelp, surfgrass, sargasso weed, coralline red algae, rockweed, various limpets, acorn barnacles, rockweed, tegula snails, hermit crabs, purple and red sea urchins

OF SPECIAL INTEREST: spectacular masses of sand castle worms, abundant ochre sea stars

PARKING/FEES: parking lot at Paradise Cove (with $5.00 fee); walk-in entry fee at Paradise Cove is $2.00; park for free in the vicinity of Dume Cove along side streets where signs indicating legal parking are posted (e.g. on Dume Dr. north of Sea Lion Pl.)

ACCESS: a long but easy walk along beach from Paradise Cove to Dume Cove (recommended access); another less desirable access is the long, steep dirt pathway at Dume Cove

CAUTIONS: none if you use the Paradise Cove access; the path down to the beach at Dume Cove is very long and steep; some of the rocks are slippery

FACILITIES: restaurant, pier, telephones, restrooms at the parking lot at Paradise Cove; none at Dume Cove.

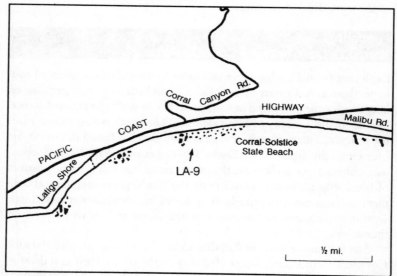

MAP 23

Locality LA-9
Corral-Solstice State Beach (See Map 23)

You will need a negative tide to see the isolated boulders here. During a very low tide, walk to the more diverse and rich tidepools west of the beach. Be sure to time your walk carefully if the tide is not very low; dangerous surf hits the point at the west end of Corral-Solstice State Beach. You may prefer to access these more western tidepools via a path located along Latigo Shore Dr. A gate in a chain link fence marks the location of this path.

RATING: 1-2

NATURE OF ROCKS: isolated boulders and cobbles

PRESENT BUT NOT ABUNDANT: California mussels, leaf barnacles, anemones, sand castle worms, feather boa kelp, striped shore crabs, coralline red algae

PARKING/FEES: along Pacific Coast Highway; no fees

ACCESS: easy access at Corral-Solstice State Beach; steep path between beach and Latigo Dr.

CAUTIONS: dangerous surf if you walk to tidepools northwest of Corral-Solstice State Beach

FACILITIES: portable bathrooms, lifeguards.

Locality LA-10
Puerco Beach to Amarillo Beach (See Map 24)

Several rocky tidepools appear along the beach although public access is limited (see Access below). The tidepools are better at Puerco Beach at the west end of Malibu Rd. (where I have rated some of them a "4"), but bouldery pools extend along much of the beach area (ratings for these are "1"-"3"). Bouldery areas farther east along Amarillo Beach lack the diversity and richness of life typical of the Puerco Beach tidepools.

RATING: 2-4

NATURE OF ROCKS: rock benches, boulders and cobbles

ESPECIALLY ABUNDANT: aggregating anemones, large and colorful giant green anemones, California mussels, leaf barnacles, sand castle worms, purple sea urchins, ochre sea stars, feather boa kelp, surfgrass, coralline algae, various limpets, acorn barnacles, sea lettuce, chitons, striped shore crabs, California sea hares, purple olives, scaly tube snails, sargasso weed, southern sea palm

PARKING/FEES: parking along Malibu Rd.; no fees

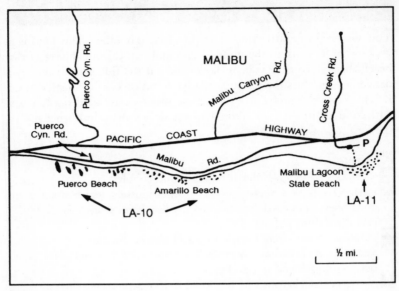

MAP 24

🗔 ACCESS: there are gated stairways in the following block numbers on Malibu Rd.: #25100 (just west of Puerco Cyn. Rd.), #24700, #24500, #24400, and #24300; you may also walk from Corral-Solstice State Beach.

🛇 CAUTIONS: slippery cobbles

🏛 FACILITIES: none; portable bathrooms and lifeguard services at nearby Corral-Solstice State Beach (see description above).

Locality LA-11
Malibu Lagoon State Beach (See Map 24)

A large cobbly area near Malibu Lagoon has some sparse tidepool life. Although the tidepools are not worth the trip, the nearby Malibu Lagoon is. The pathway to the beach (and tidepools) provides a close look at one of the few large natural lagoons remaining in Los Angeles County. Signs along the way provide information on the various life found in the lagoon. Public parking at the state beach lot is found at the corner of Pacific Coast Highway and Cross Creek Rd. If you don't wish to pay the fee, park along Pacific Coast Highway and enter via an inconspicuous (but public) access at the west end of the bridge just east of Cross Creek Rd.

RATING: less than 1

NATURE OF ROCKS: cobbles

PRESENT BUT NOT ABUNDANT: scaly tube snails, sand castle worms, acorn barnacles, coralline algae, anemones, chitons, limpets, sea hares, purple olives, tegulas, hermit crabs, rockweed, sargasso weed

PARKING/FEES: state beach parking lot (with entry fee); along Pacific Coast Highway with no fee

ACCESS: pleasant walk through a large, natural lagoon

CAUTIONS: cobbles are slippery

FACILITIES: portable bathrooms along walk to beach; lifeguards on beach.

Locality LA-12
Big Rock Beach (See Map 25)

A gated public access to Big Rock Beach is located in the 19900 block of Pacific Coast Highway. Tidepools extend to both the southeast and northwest. The extensive tidepools are made up boulders, cobbly pools and a few rock benches. Some of the most interesting life is in the low intertidal where ochre sea stars, sponges, and sea urchins flourish, so be sure to visit during a low tide.

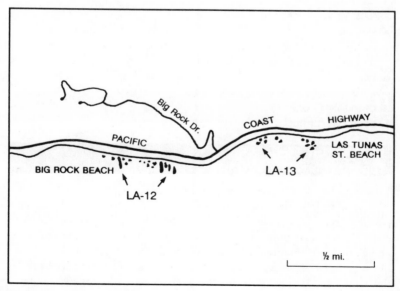

MAP 25

RATING: 2½

NATURE OF ROCKS: cobbles, boulders and a few rock benches

ESPECIALLY ABUNDANT: giant green anemones, aggregating anemones, California mussels, leaf barnacles, ochre sea stars, purple olives, sand castle worms, California sea hares, sponges, periwinkles, limpets, acorn barnacles, feather boa kelp, surfgrass, coralline algae, surfgrass, southern sea palm

OF SPECIAL INTEREST: ochre sea stars and sponges

PARKING/FEES: parking along Pacific Coast Highway; no fees

ACCESS: public access in the 19900 block of Pacific Coast Highway; short walk to beach

CAUTIONS: cobbles are slippery

FACILITIES: none.

Locality LA-13
Las Tunas State Beach (See Map 25)

Sparse boulders along Las Tunas State Beach show multitudes of California mussels, leaf barnacles, sand castle worms, feather boa kelp and other life. Access is easy with parking along Pacific Coast Highway.

RATING: 1

NATURE OF ROCKS: boulders

ESPECIALLY ABUNDANT: California mussels, leaf barnacles, sand castle worms, various limpets, aggregating anemones, feather boa kelp, sea lettuce, purple olives

PARKING/FEES: parking along Pacific Coast Highway; no fees

ACCESS: easy walk from parking lot

CAUTIONS: none

FACILITIES: none.

Locality LA-14
Topanga Canyon State Beach (See Map 26)

This state beach is located just west of Topanga Canyon Blvd. and has two parking lots; the lower one is for the handicapped. Both charge a parking fee. The cobbly tidepools are an ideal place to see plentiful examples of scaly tube snails, sand castle worms, coralline red algae and giant green anemones. Pools and low intertidal areas harbor masses of sargasso weed, surfgrass and feather boa kelp. The diversity of life is low, but what is there is quite abundant. Beware of slippery cobbles.

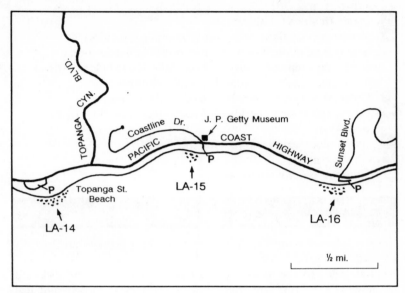

MAP 26

RATING: 1½
NATURE OF ROCKS: cobbles
ESPECIALLY ABUNDANT: sand castle worms, scaly tube snails, coralline red algae, giant green anemones, sargasso weed, surfgrass, feather boa kelp, sea lettuce, limpets
OF SPECIAL INTEREST: very nice scaly tube snails
PARKING/FEES: parking lot at park with fee; also a lower lot is provided for the handicapped
ACCESS: short walk from lot
CAUTIONS: cobbles are slippery
FACILITIES: public bathrooms, showers, drinking fountain, lifeguard services.

Locality LA-15
Coastline Dr. (See Map 26)

This small bouldery tidepool area is near the J. Paul Getty Museum on Pacific Coast Highway. As you approach the jutting line of boulders, be sure to search the nearby rocks. They are covered with huge masses of sand castle worms and giant green anemones are common on the bigger boulders. Although the area is small, the rocks are literally covered with life.

RATING: 1½

NATURE OF ROCKS: boulders

ESPECIALLY ABUNDANT: giant green anemones, California mussels, sand castle worms, feather boa kelp, sea lettuce, aggregating anemones, purple olives, coralline red algae, striped shore crabs, limpets, volcano barnacles, chitons

OF SPECIAL INTEREST: very nice sand castle worms

PARKING/FEES: small parking lot just east of Coastline Dr.; no fees

ACCESS: short walk from parking lot

CAUTIONS: none

FACILITIES: portable bathrooms.

Locality LA-16
Sunset Blvd. (See Map 26)

Scattered boulders at the eastern end of the tidepools are literally covered with sand castle worms. The masses resemble huge hornets' nests attached to the rocks. As you move farther west, the rocks off "Gladstone's 4 Fish" are covered with California mussels and leaf barnacles. Although the tidepool life is not diverse, what occurs is very abundant.

RATING: 1½

NATURE OF ROCKS: boulders, cobbles

ESPECIALLY ABUNDANT: scaly tube snails, sand castle worms, coralline red algae, feather boa kelp, California sea hares, giant green anemones, various limpets, acorn barnacles, striped shored crabs, California mussels, leaf barnacles, surfgrass, purple olives, aggregating anemones

OF SPECIAL INTEREST: large masses of sand castle worms

PARKING/FEES: large parking lot at corner of Sunset Blvd. with fee; also free parking along Pacific Coast Highway

ACCESS: steep but short pathway from parking lot at corner of Sunset Blvd.

CAUTIONS: none

FACILITIES: none, but numerous restaurants and service stations found nearby

PALOS VERDES PENINSULA

[At low tide, you can walk nearly the entire extent of the Palos Verdes Peninsula (see detail map below), starting at Flat Rock Point and continuing through the Palos Verdes Estates Shoreline Preserve, past Lunada Bay to Point Vicente. Along the way, you will encounter intermittent beaches and coves. Although the tidepools are not continuous, this is one of the longest walks along the Southern California coastline where you will find unusually extensive tidepools. The diversity and richness of life increases toward the southern end.]

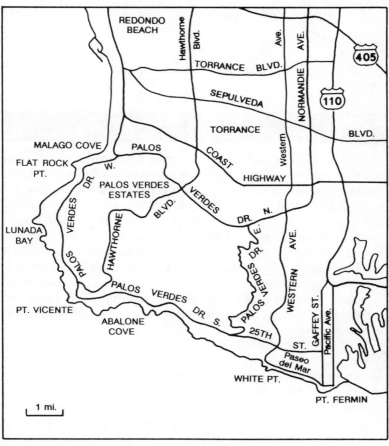

Detail of Palos Verdes Peninsula.

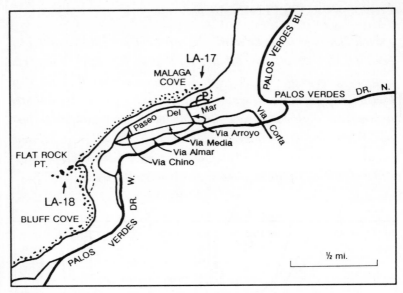

MAP 27

Locality LA-17
Malaga Cove (See Map 27)

The easiest access to Malaga Cove is by the paved pathway at the end of a large parking lot just north of the corner of Via Arroyo and Paseo Del Mar. Another access is a steep path at the corner of Via Chino and Paseo Del Mar, but is not recommended unless you are with a friend and in good shape. No matter which access you take, you will have to traverse over very slippery cobbles and boulders to reach the tidepools. Considering the difficulty in access (even the paved path presents lots of cobbles), Malaga Cove is disappointing. Surprisingly, you find little diversity here. At the north end, sand castle worms are particularly abundant, and as you move south, you will find more purple sea urchins. Hermit crabs, tegula snails and various types of limpets thrive among the cobbles.

 RATING: 2

NATURE OF ROCKS: cobbles, boulders

ESPECIALLY ABUNDANT: sand castle worms, purple sea urchins, hermit crabs, tegula snails, various limpets, volcano barnacles, spongeweed, sea bubble, surfgrass, feather boa kelp, coralline red algae, sargasso weed

PARKING/FEES: large parking lot just north of the corner of Via Arroyo and Paseo Del Mar; also street parking for second access along Paseo Del Mar; no fees

ACCESS: paved pathway at the north end of large parking lot; another access is a very steep path at the corner of Via Chino and Paseo Del Mar (not recommended)

CAUTIONS: cobbles are very slippery

FACILITIES: none except at Roessler Memorial Swimming Pool (at the north end of the cove), open to the public during summer months.

Locality LA-18
Flat Rock Point (See Map 27)

To visit the tidepools at Flat Rock Point and Bluff Cove to the south, you must follow a long, dirt pathway located off Paseo Del Mar just south of Via Almar. This is an isolated area, so be sure to bring a friend along. The tidepools here consist mostly of slippery boulders. Tidepool life here is not especially abundant or diverse. However, in some of the larger shallow pools, you will see hundreds of purple sea urchins among clumps of sargasso weed, surfgrass and other plant life. Many of the rocks have large masses of scaly tube snails attached to them.

RATING: 2

NATURE OF ROCKS: large rock outcrops, boulders, cobbles

ESPECIALLY ABUNDANT: tegula snails, hermit crabs, aggregating anemones, striped shore crabs, purple sea urchins, sargasso weed, surfgrass, feather boa kelp, coralline red algae, scaly tube snails, chitons, limpets, periwinkles, rockweed, giant green anemones

PARKING/FEES: street parking along Paseo Del Mar; no fees

ACCESS: long dirt pathway located off of Paseo Del Mar just south of Via Almar

CAUTIONS: isolated area; rocks are slippery

FACILITIES: none.

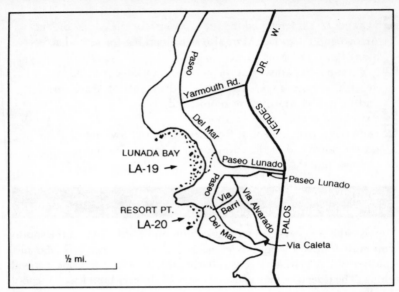

MAP 28

Locality LA-19
Lunada Bay (See Map 28)

Along Paseo Del Mar, you will find a long, dirt pathway leading down to the tidepools at the south end of Lunada Bay. This path is quite steep, so be careful. At the base of the path, you must traverse over lots of cobbles before arriving at the tidepools. Rockweed is so abundant that it literally covers most of the rocks. You won't find much diversity here beyond a variety of limpets. If you look closely, you will see scaly tube snails attached to the sides of the flatter rocks.

RATING: 2

NATURE OF ROCKS: cobbles and boulders

ESPECIALLY ABUNDANT: rockweed, a variety of limpets, tegula snails, hermit crabs, purple olives, scaly tube snails, volcano barnacles, southern sea palm, sargasso weed

OF SPECIAL INTEREST: nice scaly tube snails

PARKING/FEES: street parking along Paseo Del Mar

ACCESS: a long, steep, dirt pathway leads down to the south side of Lunada Bay

CAUTIONS: pathway is steep and slippery; cobbles are difficult to traverse

FACILITIES: none.

Locality LA-20
Resort Point (See Map 28)

At the corner of Via Barri and Paseo Del Mar a dirt pathway leads down to the center of a small cove. The path is steep with numerous switchbacks, and should only be attempted by those who are fit. Although the tidepools here are not very extensive, they are surprisingly rich, probably because it is not frequently visited. Thousands of sea urchins fill the pools. This is one of the few sites in Los Angeles County where you can see troglodyte chitons in the soft sandstone. Here you may be able to identify most of the plants and animals described in this book. Again, slippery rocks abound.

RATING: 4

NATURE OF ROCKS: rock benches, boulders and cobbles

ESPECIALLY ABUNDANT: sea urchins, ochre sea stars, California mussels, sand castle worms, chitons, wavy turbans, leaf barnacles, aggregating anemones, giant green anemones, coralline red algae, feather boa kelp, California sea hares

OF SPECIAL INTEREST: thousands of troglodyte chitons in the soft sandstone

PARKING/FEES: street parking along Via Barri and Paseo Del Mar; no fees

ACCESS: a very steep dirt pathway with numerous switchbacks leads down to the center of a small cove

CAUTIONS: this steep pathway should only be undertaken by those in good shape; also the rocks can be slippery

FACILITIES: none.

Locality LA-21
Point Vicente (See Map 29)

This is a popular fishing area with an easy (although somewhat long) pathway leading down to the cove south of Point Vicente. At the base of the pathway are numerous cobbles which you must walk over before getting to the tidepools. The rocks here are not extensive, but in this limited area there is an abundance of diverse life. Be careful, because the rocks can be slippery.

RATING: 3½

NATURE OF ROCKS: rock benches, boulders and cobbles

ESPECIALLY ABUNDANT: acorn barnacles, limpets, periwinkles, striped shored crabs, tegulas and hermit crabs, sea urchins, California sea hares, coralline red algae, giant green anemones,

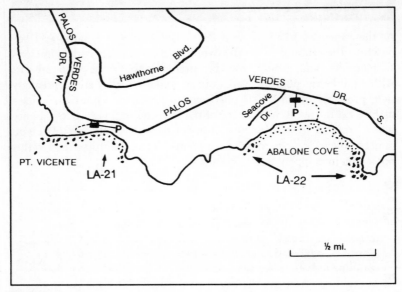

MAP 29

sargasso weed, sand castle worms, scaly tube snails, California mussels, leaf barnacles, volcano barnacles

PARKING/FEES: small parking lot off of Palos Verdes Dr.; no fees

ACCESS: long, easy path leading from the north end of the parking lot

CAUTIONS: rocks are slippery

FACILITIES: public restrooms, drinking fountain.

Locality LA-22
Abalone Cove (See Map 29)

Along Palos Verdes Dr., southeast of Seacove Dr., is a large parking lot and a long, dirt pathway leading down to Abalone Cove. Although there are tidepools at the northwest end, those at the southeast end are the most extensive and commonly visited. You'll find a variety of habitats, ranging from boulders and cobbles to flat rocks, with intermittent shallow pools. Tidepool life is similarly rich in diversity and numbers. If you spend some time here, you will probably be able to find most of the plants and animals in this book. However, its long and rather difficult access lowers its rating from "5" to "4."

RATING: 4

NATURE OF ROCKS: rock benches, boulders and cobbles

ESPECIALLY ABUNDANT: sand castle worms, California sea hares, sea urchins (both red and purple), giant green anemones, ochre sea stars, California mussels, leaf barnacles, aggregating anemones, limpets, a variety of barnacles, periwinkles, tegulas, hermit crabs, sargasso weed, coralline red algae

OF SPECIAL INTEREST: ochre sea stars are particularly abundant in the low intertidal zone

PARKING/FEES: large parking lot with fee

ACCESS: very long pathway that is somehat difficult because of the cobbly beach that must be crossed to access the tidepools

CAUTIONS: cobbles are difficult to walk across; path is very long and somewhat isolated

FACILITIES: portable bathrooms at parking lot.

Locality LA-23
Paseo Del Mar (See Map 30)

Tidepools along the coastline here are extensive, but you must follow a long dirt pathway. Although a chainlink fence occurs in this area, it is down in one section, and open to the public. If you walk toward the

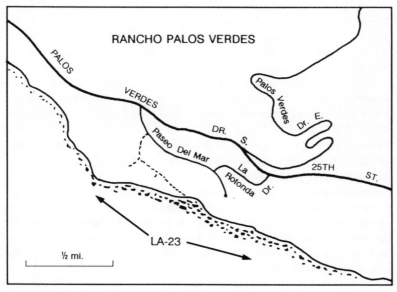

MAP 30

cliffs from the fence, the path will split in two directions; take the southeastern path and you will see the pathway that leads down to the cobbly beach with its slippery rocks. Tidepools here are a mixture of gently dipping rock layers and boulders. Although life is diverse, the abundance is fairly low.

RATING: 3

NATURE OF ROCKS: gently dipping rock layers and boulders

ESPECIALLY ABUNDANT: periwinkles, limpets, chitons, acorn barnacles, tegula snails, hermit crabs, purple sea urchins, sand castle worms, coralline red algae, California sea hares, California mussels, ochre sea stars, giant green anemones

OF SPECIAL INTEREST: in the lower rock layers, there is a soft sandstone with thousands of troglodyte chitons in oval depressions

PARKING/FEES: street parking along Paseo Del Mar; no fees

ACCESS: long dirt pathway leading down to a cobbly beach; be sure to take the left branch of the path at the top of the cliffs

CAUTIONS: area is isolated; cobbles are slippery

FACILITIES: none.

Locality LA-24
White Point (See Map 31)

The best tidepools on the Palos Verdes Peninsula are located at White Point. Access is easy, with parking next to the tidepools. These pools are rich with a diversity of life, making White Point a photographer's dream. Many of the photographs in this book were taken here. As you explore the rocky point adjacent to the parking lot, you may notice the remains of an old structure that was once a Japanese resort hotel called White Point Hot Springs. The bathhouse was heated by hot springs generated from offshore geothermal vents. Some pools have a strong sulfur smell and are filled with a white "scum." This is a white bacteria that thrives on the sulfur discharged through the springs. Unfortunately, the tidepool life is harmed by the high sulfur content, so you must venture seaward to see more life.

Farther out, the tidepools consist of table-like rocks with deep, intermittent crevices. Ochre sea stars cling to the rocks here, especially in the surf zone. Be careful of the strong surf if you venture to the seaward edge of the tidepools. Sea urchins are also common here, as well as other tidepool animals and plants. You may see large sea cucumbers here as well.

If you visit the southernmost part of White Point, pay particular

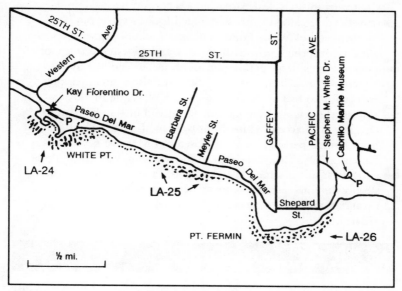

MAP 31

attention to the rocks that make up the tidepools. The layers have been intensely folded, and these folds so completely enclose water that the water in adjacent pools may be at different levels during low tide. People familiar with geology will recognize one of these folds as a "plunging anticline" that has been eroded so that the rocks forming the folds are nearly vertical (and difficult to traverse). The pools are deep and offer a colorful assortment of tidepool life. Some of the rocks harbor thousands of troglodyte chitons in oval-shaped depressions. As you move farther south, there is a more protected cove (with a separate access) where the rock layers are nearly vertical. The softer layers of rock have weathered away, forming deep grooves parallel to the harder layers. Abundant and diverse tidepool life thrives in these tidepools. If you spend enough time at White Point, you'll surely see most of the plants and animals described in this book.

RATING: 5

NATURE OF ROCKS: flat to steeply dipping rock benches, boulders and cobbles

ESPECIALLY ABUNDANT: ochre sea stars, purple and red sea urchins, giant green anemones, California sea hares, various limpets, barnacles, troglodyte chitons, aggregating anemones, coralline red algae, feather boa kelp, sand castle worms, California mussels, leaf barnacles, sea cucumbers

OF SPECIAL INTEREST: intensely folded rock layers at the southern end of White Point; remains of an old Japanese resort with sulfur springs; general abundance and diversity of tidepool life

PARKING/FEES: large parking lot (with fee) at end of Kay Fiorentino Dr. which closes at 5:30 P.M.; also a small parking area (with no fee) at the cove just south of White Pt.

ACCESS: short walk from parking lot at end of Kay Fiorentino Dr.; may also access White Point by way of a path which leads from a small parking lot along Paseo Del Mar just south of Kay Fiorentino Dr. This path leads to the cove south of White Point

CAUTIONS: surf is strong at the seaward faces of the rocks; the steeply dipping rock layers are difficult to traverse

FACILITIES: restrooms, drinking fountains; showers; lifeguard services.

Locality LA-25
Barbara St. to Meyler St. (See Map 31)

Extensive tidepools are found along Paseo Del Mar between White Point and Point Fermin. Two good pathways lead down to the rocky beach; one at the end of Barbara St. and another at the end of Meyler St. A nice way to visit these tidepools is to enter by one path and leave by the other, exploring the tidepools in between. Both pathways are paved. The tidepools, although extensive, are not as diverse as other Palos Verdes locations. Although the water in this embayment is often silty, this is a rewarding tidepool area and well worth seeing. When I visited, I was lucky to spot a large striped sea slug, 5 inches long and a half inch across.

RATING: 3

NATURE OF ROCKS: boulders, cobbles and flat rock benches

ESPECIALLY ABUNDANT: chitons, giant green anemones, feather boa kelp, coralline red algae, nice sand castle worms, sea urchins, California sea hares, sargaasso weed, California mussels, leaf barnacles, volcano barnacles, surfgrass

PARKING/FEES: street parking along Paseo Del Mar; no fees

ACCESS: two paved pathways along Paleo Del Mar: one at Barbara St. and one at Meyler St.

CAUTIONS: rocks can be slippery

FACILITIES: public restrooms and a drinking fountain at the Meyler St. access.

Locality LA-26
Cabrillo State Beach Pt. Fermin (See Map 31)

The Cabrillo Marine Museum at the beach park is an excellent place to see many of the tidepool plants and animals inhabiting our coastline. The museum houses aquarium tanks, tidepool exhibits and tours, as well as a tidepool touch tank. The museum is free (but with a parking fee), and is closed on Monday. By walking toward Pt. Fermin from the beach park, you may explore the tidepools along most of the the point below the lighthouse. It is often windy here which causes the surf to hit the northwestern end of the point with great force. As you approach the tidepools, you will see a wall with paintings of various tidepool creatures. It is used by the museum personnel conducting tours along the tidepools. The nearby Pt. Fermin Park is a pleasant picnic place.

RATING: 3

NATURE OF ROCKS: cobbles and boulders

ESPECIALLY ABUNDANT: acorn barnacles, limpets, tegulas, hermit crabs, aggregating anemones, giant green anemones, nice sand castle worms, scaly tube snails, sea urchins, sargasso weed, surfgrass

PARKING/FEES: parking at museum with fee; or may park for free on street along Stephen M. White Dr.

ACCESS: walk toward Pt. Fermin from Cabrillo State Beach

CAUTIONS: cobbles are very slippery; surf at Fermin Point can be quite forceful

FACILITIES: public restrooms and drinking fountain at the museum as well as a gift shop.

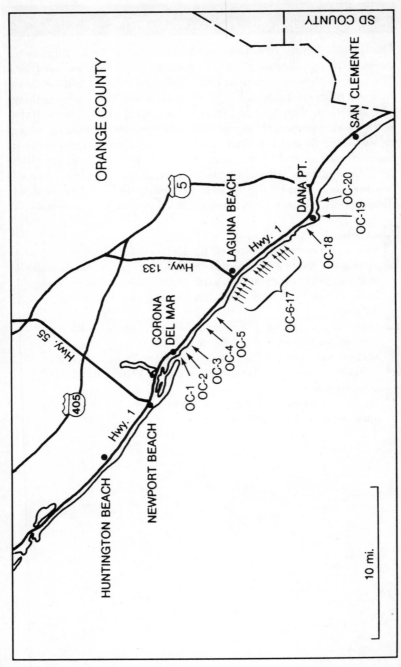

MAP 32

Orange County

The tidepools in Orange County (see Map 32) are clustered along the coast from Corona Del Mar to Dana Point. The area near Laguna has long been a popular place for tidepool excursions.

CORONA DEL MAR TO REEF POINT

[One of the most interesting features about the tidepools at Corona Del Mar and the locality just south (OC-2) are the intensely folded rocks, particularly noticable in the cliffs. Tidepool life is rich and diverse at Corona Del Mar but diminishes as you move south to the sandy beaches of Pelican Point (OC-3) and Reef Point (OC-4).]

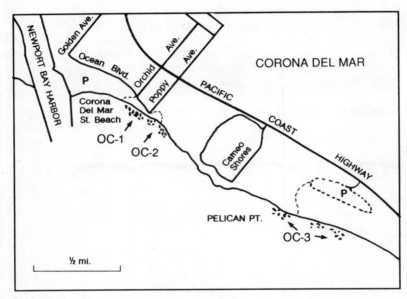

MAP 33

Locality OC-1
Corona Del Mar State Beach (See Map 33)

The tidepools are south of the state beach in a nice protected cove. The tidepools are not only extensive but are also filled with an abundance of diverse plants and animals. The rock layers are nearly vertical here and therefore craggy. Slippery boulders make these tidepools somewhat difficult to get around.

 RATING: 3½

NATURE OF ROCKS: craggy rocks with nearly vertical layers, boulders and cobbles

ESPECIALLY ABUNDANT: aggregating anemones, giant green anemones, California mussels, leaf barnacles, sand castle worms, giant owl limpets, feather boa kelp, acorn barnacles, scaly tube snails, coralline red algae, tegula snails, hermit crabs, red and purple sea urchins, chitons, striped shore crabs

PARKING/FEES: parking lot (with fee) at Corona Del Mar State Beach; also street parking on Orchid Ave. and Ocean Blvd.

ACCESS: may access by walking south from the Corona Del Mar State Beach, or by a long paved pathway leading down from the corner of Orchid Ave. and Ocean Blvd.

CAUTIONS: rocks are very slippery

FACILITIES: lifeguard services, public restrooms, drinking fountains, showers, and a snack bar

Locality OC-2
Poppy Ave. (See Map 33)

This small sandy cove has tidepools both to the north and south. The northern pools are interesting because of the intensely folded layers that make up the rocks on the beach and in the cliffs. Be sure you take time to appreciate this interesting geological formation. The tidepools both north and south of the cove are filled with an abundance of diverse tidepool life. Many of the rocks are covered with algae (especially seaward due to the surf spray) and can be quite slippery.

RATING: 3½

NATURE OF ROCKS: rock layers that may be steeply or gently dipping in different places

ESPECIALLY ABUNDANT: sargasso weed, spongeweed, surfgrass, sea bubble, tegula snails, coralline red algae, feather boa kelp, sand castle worms, leaf barnacles, giant green anemones, limpets, chitons, acorn barnacles, surfgrass, California mussels, sea urchins

OF SPECIAL INTEREST: intensely folded rock layers

PARKING/FEES: along the nearby streets; no fees

ACCESS: a long paved pathway located at the corner where Ocean Blvd. deadends into Poppy Ave. leads down to a small, sandy cove

CAUTIONS: many rocks are covered with algae and are very slippery

FACILITIES: lifeguard services, public restrooms, showers and a drinking fountain (found on the path above the beach)

Locality OC-3
Pelican Point (See Map 33)

The large park on top of the cliffs is isolated but has some good bike paths and hiking trails. Several pathways lead to the beach area, although I recommend the path leading from the northernmost parking area. No matter which path you choose, you'll be faced with a long walk. The tidepools are somewhat sparse and surrounded with lots of sand and harbor masses of sand castle worms. If you look carefully under the rock overhangs, you will likely see some velvety red sponges. When I visited this locality, I saw a giant keyhole limpet in one of the isolated pools. However, in general the diversity of life here is low, and the number of organisms is low as well.

RATING: 3

NATURE OF ROCKS: rock benches, boulders, cobbles

ESPECIALLY ABUNDANT: sand castle worms, rockweed, aggregating anemones, leaf barnacles, California mussels, acorn barnacles, feather boa kelp, surfgrass, volcano barnacles, coralline red algae, velvety red sponges, nice giant green anemones, giant keyhole limpets

OF SPECIAL INTEREST: nice sand castle worms, velvety red sponges

PARKING/FEES: large parking lots; no fees

ACCESS: several pathways lead down to the beach area; the path leading from the northernmost parking area accesses the better tidepools

CAUTIONS: isolated area

FACILITIES: public restrooms, showers, and drinking fountains in the park above the beach

Locality OC-4
Crystal Cove State Beach (See Map 34)

Parking for Crystal Cove State Beach is on the east side of Coast Highway indicated by a sign for Los Trancos Canyon. Park at the south end of the lot where a sign points to the beach access. A long paved pathway leads underneath Pacific Coast Highway. At the end of this path turn left on the paved road which winds through an old beach community and eventually to Crystal Cove State Beach. The rocks making up the tidepools are fine-grained, layered sandstones harboring an interesting variety of plants and animals. Crystal Cove is also a good beach for picnics and swimming.

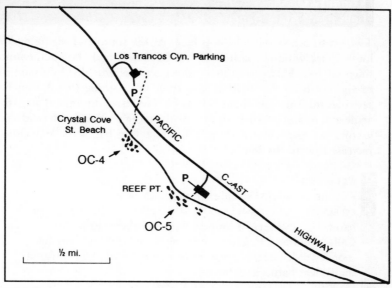

MAP 34

 RATING: 3

NATURE OF ROCKS: folded rock layers with deep round pools

ESPECIALLY ABUNDANT: numerous acorn and leaf barnacles, chitons, giant green anemones, giant owl limpets, periwinkles, California mussels, sand castle worms, aggregating anemones, volcano barnacles, feather boa kelp, sargasso weed, coralline red algae

PARKING/FEES: large parking lot on the east side of Pacific Coast Highway indicated by a sign for Los Trancos Canyon; no fees

ACCESS: a long paved pathway at the south end of the parking lot extends underneath Pacific Coast Highway; turn left on the paved road leading to Crystal Cove State Beach; tidepools are just to the south

CAUTIONS: none

FACILITIES: bathrooms, drinking fountains, dressing rooms (at parking lot), lifeguard services (on beach)

Locality OC-5
Reef Point State Beach (See Map 34)

Two paths access the tidepools here. At the south end of the parking lot a long, winding path leads to the beach and the southernmost tidepool area. However, a more direct route is provided by a path just to the north of the drive as you enter the parking lot. A sign here provides information about tidepools. The rocks dip inland at a steep angle and harbor a variety of life. At the more northern end, sand castle worms are particularly abundant while leaf barnacles and chitons increase toward the south.

RATING: 3

NATURE OF ROCKS: steeply dipping rock benches

ESPECIALLY ABUNDANT: sand castle worms, rockweed, acorn barnacles, a variety of limpets, large southern sea palms, California mussels, giant green anemones, volcano barnacles, spongeweed, surfgrass, feather boa kelp, hermit crabs, tegula snails, leaf barnacles, chitons

PARKING/FEES: large parking lot with fee

ACCESS: most direct access is provided by a path just to the north of the drive as you enter the parking lot; another is via a long, winding path leading from the southern end of the parking lot to the beach

CAUTIONS: isolated during winter months

FACILITIES: public restrooms, showers, and drinking fountains

CRESCENT BAY TO SOUTH LAGUNA

[*The tidepools here are the most numerous and diverse in Orange County. If you look closely, you will be able to find most of the plants and animals described in this book. Particularly abundant are purple sea urchins and even red sea urchins. Rocks along the coastline are fairly hard with angular fragments embedded in them. They are called breccias (pronounced "brechas") and provide an ideal attaching surface for tidepool life.*]

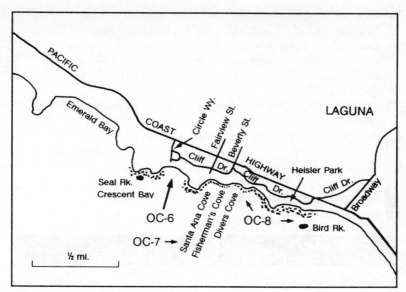

MAP 35

Locality OC-6
Crescent Bay (See Map 35)

Two fine tidepool areas are found at the northern and southern ends of Crescent Bay. At the north end of the cove, splendid tidepools extend around the point. Offshore on Seal Rock, you will hear the continuous barking of numerous seals. Good snorkeling is found in the protected cove nearby. Spectacular giant green anemones are especially prolific here, some reaching 6 inches across. At the base of the rocks, you may also see some large chitons. Although boulders abound here, the rocks are not slippery.

South of the cove lie more extensive tidepools. This area is also accessible from Santa Ana Cove to the south (see the description of locality OC-7). This tidepool rates a "5" because of the diversity and abundance of life. Sand castle worms have formed massive clumps on the sides of the rocks, and edges of individual tubes extend out from the rest of the mass. This is also a fine place for bird-watching. If you continue around the point, you will find yourself in Santa Ana Cove, described below.

RATING: 4-5

NATURE OF ROCKS: rock benches, boulders and cobbles

✖ ESPECIALLY ABUNDANT: sand castle worms, aggregating anemones, California mussels, leaf barnacles, giant green anemones, chitons, purple sea urchins, giant owl limpets, volcano barnacles, striped shore crabs, coralline red algae, feather boa kelp, spongeweed, surfgrass, sea lettuce, rockweed, acorn barnacles

🐚 OF SPECIAL INTEREST: very large giant green anemones and chitons

🏖 PARKING/FEES: along nearby streets; no fees

📖 ACCESS: access this cove either by a stairway at the north end of Circle Way, or by another stairway at the corner of Cliff Dr. and Circle Way

⚠ CAUTIONS: rocks can be slippery

🏛 FACILITIES: none

Locality OC-7
Santa Ana Cove/Fisherman's Cove (See Map 35)

Tidepools at the north end of Santa Ana Cove are quite large and extend around the point into Crescent Bay. At the south end is another set of tidepools that contains a rich diversity of life. Look under the overhanging rocks and you will see bat stars and ochre sea stars as well as sponges. As you move farther south, the rocks become flatter with shallow pools where purple sea urchins flourish. If you follow the tidepools around the point, you will come upon a smaller cove. This is Fisherman's Cove with no public access except by walking south from Santa Ana Cove. This small but attractive area offers you a selection of sea shells washed upon the beach including polished shells of wavy turbans. At the south end of Fisherman's Cove you'll find a small rocky area that provides an excellent place to safely observe low intertidal habitats when the tides are very low (preferably negative). Purple sea urchins and red sea urchins are especially abundant.

✖ RATING: 4-5

▦ NATURE OF ROCKS: rock benches, boulders and cobbles

✖ ESPECIALLY ABUNDANT: sponges, bat stars, ochre sea stars, sponges, California mussels, leaf barnacles, acorn barnacles, sand castle worms, feather boa kelp, spongeweed, giant green anemones, large chitons, California sea hares, tegula snails, hermit crabs, purple and red sea urchins

🐚 OF SPECIAL INTEREST: abundant sponges, sea stars, and sea urchins

🏖 PARKING/FEES: street parking along Cliff Dr. and Fairview St.; no fees

≣ ACCESS: a stairway at the corner of Fairview St. and Cliff Dr. leads down to Santa Ana Cove

⊻ CAUTIONS: none

🏛 FACILITIES: lifeguard services, phone at top of stairs

Locality OC-8
Heisler Park (Divers Cove to Bird Rock) (See Map 35)

Tidepools are very popular in Laguna Beach. Diverse habitats ranging from boulders to flat rocks with intermittent pools make this a haven for a wide range of plants and animals. You can safely explore the low intertidal zone during a low tide. Be careful when walking on rocks covered with slippery feather boa kelp. In the low intertidal zone, look for thousands of chitons burrowed in the rocks. Bird-watching is rewarding here. Laguna Beach itself is a fun place to visit with its numerous restaurants, art museums and gift shops.

 RATING: 4-5

 NATURE OF ROCKS: flat rock benches, boulders and cobbles

🕱 ESPECIALLY ABUNDANT: volcano barnacles, coralline red algae, spongeweed, feather boa kelp, California mussels, leaf barnacles, sand castle worms, sea urchins, California sea hares, aggregating anemones, giant green anemones, sargasso weed, surfgrass

▤ PARKING/FEES: ample street parking, although much is metered

≣ ACCESS: numerous stairways lead down to the tidepools along Heisler Park

⊻ CAUTIONS: rocks covered with feather boa kelp are very slippery

🏛 FACILITIES: restrooms, showers, drinking fountains, lifeguard services; also nearby restaurants, art museums and gift shops

Locality OC-9
Cheney's Point (See Map 36)

Two stairways access the tidepools here: one at the northern end of Sleepy Hollow Lane, and another at the end of Cleo Street. A small, rocky area lies between. The most abundant organisms here are aggregating anemones, California mussels, acorn barnacles and sand castle worms. Common plants include feather boa kelp, spongeweed and coralline algae. As in other sandy areas, purple olives are common.

 RATING: 2

 NATURE OF ROCKS: cobbles and boulders

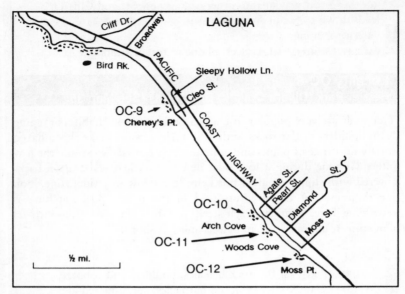

MAP 36

⊠ ESPECIALLY ABUNDANT: aggregating anemones, California mussels, acorn barnacles, sand castle worms, volcano barnacles, limpets, leaf barnacles, coralline red algae, giant green anemones, feather boa kelp, spongeweed

⛴ PARKING/FEES: parking is limited to nearby streets; no fees

⛴ ACCESS: two stairways access the tidepools: one at the northern end of Sleepy Hollow Lane, and one at the end of Cleo St.

📛 CAUTIONS: none

🏛 FACILITIES: none

Locality OC-10
Arch Cove (See Map 36)

A stairway at the end of Agate St. leads down to a beach with two, small rocky areas. The rocks are covered with algae and are slippery. The most interesting organisms are sand castle worms which cover the sides of some of the rocks. There are also abundant purple olives. To the south looms a rocky point with an archway leading to Woods Cove (described below).

⊠ RATING: 1

⊠ NATURE OF ROCKS: boulders, cobbles and rock benches

■ ESPECIALLY ABUNDANT: sand castle worms, purple olives, coralline red algae, giant green anemones, barnacles (both volcano and acorn), rough limpets, California mussels, leaf barnacles, feather boa kelp

■ PARKING/FEES: street parking; no fees

■ ACCESS: stairway leads down to beach; you must make a small jump at the end of the stairs

■ CAUTIONS: slippery algae-covered rocks

■ FACILITIES: none

Locality OC-11
Woods Cove (See Map 36)

Two stairways access the tidepools here: one on Ocean Way between Pearl St. and Diamond St. (preferred), or another at the end of Diamond St. The tidepools are limited, both in size and diversity of life.

■ RATING: 2

■ NATURE OF ROCKS: rock benches, boulders and cobbles

■ ESPECIALLY ABUNDANT: acorn barnacles, California mussels, limpets, rockweed, leaf barnacles, pink encrusting coralline algae

■ PARKING/FEES: parking on nearby streets; no fees

■ ACCESS: two accesses: a stairway on Ocean Way between Pearl St. and Diamond St. (preferred), and another stairway at the end of Diamond St.

■ CAUTIONS: rocks are slippery

■ FACILITIES: lifeguard services

Locality OC-12
Moss Point (See Map 36)

A stairway at the end of Moss St. leads to a small, rocky tidepool area largely composed of boulders and cobbles, with organisms typical of this habitat: a variety of limpets, barnacles (both acorn and volcano), striped shore crabs, tegula snails and hermit crabs. The pools contain giant green anemones, California sea hares, feather boa kelp and coralline red algae. Rockweed is also common.

■ RATING: 2

■ NATURE OF ROCKS: rock benches, boulders and cobbles

■ ESPECIALLY ABUNDANT: limpets, barnacles (both acorn and

volcano), striped shore crabs, tegula snails, hermit crabs, California sea hares, feather boa kelp, coralline red algae, rockweed

PARKING/FEES: parking along nearby streets; no fees
ACCESS: stairway at the end of Moss St. leads to tidepools
CAUTIONS: none
FACILITIES: lifeguard services

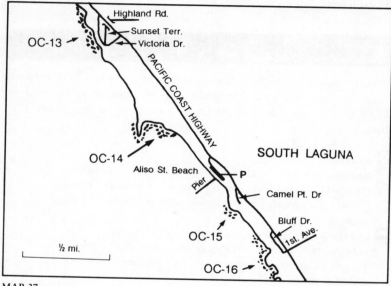

MAP 37

Locality OC-13
Sunset Terrace (See Map 37)

This large rocky area begins just north of a public stairway at the end of Sunset Terrace. Be sure the tide is low (close to 0.0 ft.) so you can appreciate some of the more interesting life here. Especially impressive are masses of sand castle worms that cover the sides of the rocks. Rockweed covers many of the rocks, making them slippery. Also, be wary of the unstable cliffs here.

RATING: 4
NATURE OF ROCKS: rock benches and boulders
ESPECIALLY ABUNDANT: small acorn barnacles, California mussels, giant green anemones, purple sea urchins, surfgrass,

feather boa kelp, coralline red algae, rockweed, sand castle worms, volcano barnacles, limpets

PARKING/FEES: parking on nearby streets; no fees

ACCESS: a public stairway at the end of Sunset Terrace leads to the beach; tidepools are just north of this stairway

CAUTIONS: cliffs are unstable; some rocks are very slippery

FACILITIES: lifeguard services

Locality OC-14
Aliso State Beach (See Map 37)

Tidepools here are some distance north of Aliso State Beach, but the walk is well worth it, for the pools are rich with life. Shallow pools on top of the flat rocks harbor hundreds of purple sea urchins and brightly colored giant green anemones, giving the impression of an underwater flower garden. You might even see red sea urchins here. Aliso State Beach is also a pleasant place to visit with ample facilities and a pier for fishing. A trailer park occupies the cliffs above, but the access from this park is private.

RATING: 5

NATURE OF ROCKS: rock benches

ESPECIALLY ABUNDANT: California mussels, small acorn barnacles, purple sea urchins, giant green anemones, red sea urchins, coralline red algae, spongeweed, rockweed, volcano barnacles, velvety red sponges, surfgrass, leaf barnacles, sand castle worms, sargasso weed, various chitons, giant owl limpets, periwinkles, striped shore crabs

PARKING/FEES: large parking lot at Aliso Beach Park provides metered parking

ACCESS: long but easy walk north from Aliso State Beach

CAUTIONS: none

FACILITIES: public restrooms, showers, drinking fountains, telephones, lifeguard services

Locality OC-15
South of Camel Pt. Dr. (See Map 37)

An enticing beach awaits you at the base of a stairway along Pacific Coast Highway between Camel Pt. Dr. and Bluff Dr., with many cement barbecue pits. The tidepools are north of this beach. Although large, the tidepool habitats are not as diverse as other Laguna localities. Especially interesting are the velvety red sponges on rocks in the wetter areas.

RATING: 3

NATURE OF ROCKS: rock benches and boulders

ESPECIALLY ABUNDANT: California mussels, leaf barnacles, sponges, anemones (both giant and aggregating), volcano barnacles, acorn barnacles, sea lettuce, surfgrass, coralline red algae, southern sea palm

OF SPECIAL INTEREST: velvety red sponges in the low intertidal

PARKING/FEES: parking along Pacific Coast Highway; no fees

ACCESS: public access to this tidepool is marked only by a sign saying "Pedestrian Beach Access" on the west side of Pacific Coast Highway between Camel Pt. Dr. and Bluff Dr.; may also access either by walking south from Aliso Beach park or by walking north from the Bluff Dr. locality south of here

CAUTIONS: rocks may be slippery

FACILITIES: none

Locality OC-16
Bluff Dr. (See Map 37)

A bus stop at the corner of Bluff Dr. and Pacific Coast Highway marks the location of a long public stairway which leads down to a pleasant beach area with a protected cove. A small rocky area lies south of the stairway where California mussels, leaf barnacles, sand castle worms and giant green anemones cover the rocks. Purple sea urchins flourish in the small pools on top of the rocks. Be aware of the strong surf at the seaward edge of the tidepools.

RATING: 3½

NATURE OF ROCKS: rock benches and boulders

ESPECIALLY ABUNDANT: California mussels, leaf barnacles, sand castle worms, giant green anemones, purple sea urchins, acorn and volcano barnacles, giant owl limpets, rockweed, spongeweed, coralline red algae

PARKING/FEES: parking along Pacific Coast Highway; no fees

ACCESS: long stairway at the corner of Bluff Dr. and Pacific Coast Highway; there is a bus stop at this corner

CAUTIONS: strong surf at the seaward faces of the rock benches

FACILITIES: lifeguard services

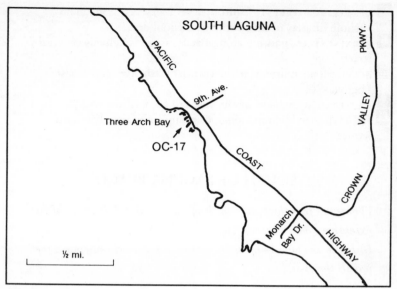

MAP 38

Locality OC-17
Thousand Steps Beach (Three Arch Bay) (See Map 38)

A stairway of 220 steps (not 1000!) begins at the corner of 9th Ave. and Pacific Coast Highway in South Laguna and leads you to the beach. Several rocky areas here are separated by sandy beaches. Sand castle worms have built impressive masses of tubes on the sides of rocks in the lower intertidal zones. Tidepools north of the stairway are more diverse and harbor California sea hares, sea stars, and giant keyhole limpets in addition to the life found farther south. You have a better chance of seeing other organisms too, such as California mussels reaching a length of 5 inches or more. The surf is quite strong on the seaward edge of the tidepools, so be careful when venturing to the outer faces of the rocks.

RATING: 4

NATURE OF ROCKS: rock benches and boulders

ESPECIALLY ABUNDANT: California mussels, acorn barnacles, leaf barnacles, California sea hares, aggregating anemones, giant keyhole limpets, sea stars, sand castle worms, variety of snails and limpets, striped shore crabs, rockweed, spongeweed, coralline red algae, sargasso weed, southern sea palm, surfgrass

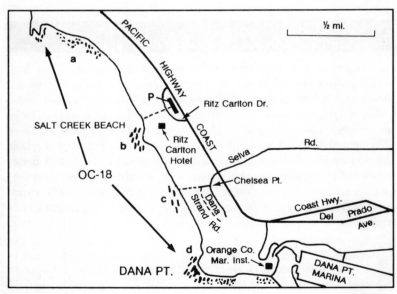

OF SPECIAL INTEREST: California sea hares, sea stars, giant keyhole limpets in the northern tidepool area

PARKING/FEES: parking along Pacific Coast Highway or nearby streets

ACCESS: long stairway at the corner of 9th Ave. and Coast Highway

CAUTIONS: strong surf at the seaward faces of the rocks

FACILITIES: public restrooms, drinking fountains, lifeguard services

SOUTH OF LAGUNA BEACH

[There are few tidepools south of Laguna Beach because of the extensive sandy beaches. However, the Orange County Marine Institute at Dana Point is the site of some lovely tidepools well worth the visit.]

MAP 39

Four distinct tidepool sites may be visited along Salt Creek Beach, with two ways to reach the beach. One is by way of a long, paved pathway at the northern end of Dana Strand Rd. A preferable route, however, is near the Ritz Carlton Hotel with a metered parking lot (strictly enforced). Across the street is a large park with extensive lawns, picnic tables, tennis courts and restrooms. Several paths lead from the main road to the beach, and any of them may be used to reach the tidepools. The most extensive tidepools are at the north end of Salt Creek Beach (OC-18a), and I have given these a rating of "3½." These habitats are quite diverse, ranging from a cobbly, bouldery area at the southern end with flat table-like rocks and shallow pools farther north. A small, sandy cove at the north end offers some empty shells of wavy turbans as well as lobster carapaces washed up on the sand. The northern edge is characterized by steep cliffs with impressive caves. Be careful of slippery boulders here.

A second tidepool site (OC-18b) is located at the base of the cliffs below the Ritz Carlton Hotel. This small area of boulders and rock outcrops displays nearly vertical layers extending away from the shoreline. Some impressive masses of sand castle worms resembling hornets' nests bulge from many of the boulders. If you look closely at the sides of the rocks, you will also see some striking clumps of scaly tube snails. Those venturing into the low intertidal will see some sponges attached to the sides of submerged rocks. Although a small tidepool, it is impressive and rates a "3".

As you continue south along Salt Creek Beach, you will encounter another small tidepool area (OC-18c) at the base of the paved path leading from Dana Strand Rd. Here the rock layers are again nearly vertical but run parallel to the beach. Because these rocks are difficult to get around, and the richness of life here is not great, I give it a rating of "1." Because the rocks are not high or extensive, you need a negative tide to be able to appreciate this tidepool area.

At the southern end of Salt Creek Beach lies another tidepool area (OC-18d) difficult to traverse due to the cliffs. However, if you venture around this point, you will see clinging to the face of the rocks good colonies of California mussels, leaf barnacles, surfgrass and coralline red algae. The water-filled crevices in the rocks harbor colorful urchins, sponges and giant green anemones. Be careful walking along the point. The rocks can be slippery, and the waves crash into the point with a great deal of force. Although the life here is rich, the rating for this tidepool area is "1" due to its limited extent, fairly low diversity and difficult access.

▨ RATING: 1-3½

▨ NATURE OF ROCKS: cliffs, rock benches, boulders, cobbles

▨ ESPECIALLY ABUNDANT: California mussels, coralline red algae, sand castle worms, limpets, leaf barnacles, California sea hares, tegulas, hermit crabs, purple and red sea urchins, giant keyhole limpets, anemones (both giant green and aggregating), rockweed, spongeweed, sargasso weed, feather boa kelp, wavy turbans, purple olives, giant owl limpets, scaly tube snails, surfgrass, sponges, ochre sea stars, acorn barnacles, chitons, striped shore crabs, periwinkles

▨ OF SPECIAL INTEREST: large numbers of wavy turban shells in northern cove (at OC-18a); beautiful masses of sand castle worms and sponges in the lower intertidal (at OC-18b)

▨ PARKING/FEES: free street parking along Dana Strand Rd. or large metered parking lot near the Ritz Carlton Hotel

▨ ACCESS: by way of a long, paved pathway at the northern end of Dana Strand Rd.; a preferable access, however, is near the Ritz Carlton Hotel from a large, metered parking lot; across the street from this lot is a large park with several paths leading to the beach

▨ CAUTIONS: many of the rock benches and boulders are slippery; surf at the seaward edges of the rocks and cliffs is very strong.

▨ FACILITIES: along the beach (especially near the Ritz Carlton Hotel), there are public restrooms, showers, drinking fountains and lifeguard services; large picnic area near the Ritz Carlton

Locality OC-19
Dana Point/Orange County Marine Institute (See Map 40)

Dana Point is a rocky headland that consists of extensive and richly diverse tidepools. They begin at the base of a stairway just north of a long jetty at the Orange County Marine Institute, and except for a small interrupting cove, extend all the way around Dana Point. Although the boulders here are difficult to traverse, they are not particularly slippery except at the southern end where algae coats them. To avoid walking over the boulders twice, you may follow a dirt pathway at the base of the cliffs and stroll north as far as you want. Then walk out to the tidepools and work your way south. But be careful, because these are unstable cliffs, and the farther north you go, the more isolated you become.

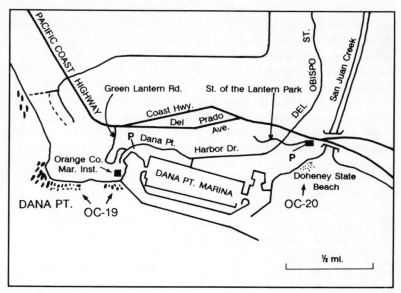

MAP 40

 RATING: 4

NATURE OF ROCKS: cobbles, boulders and rock benches farther north

ESPECIALLY ABUNDANT: California sea hares, giant green sea anemones, hermit crabs, tegula snails, acorn barnacles, variety of limpets, rockweed, feather boa kelp, surfgrass, sargasso weed, coralline red algae, aggregating anemones, California mussels, leaf barnacles

PARKING/FEES: adequate free parking in nearby lots

ACCESS: short stairway near Orange County Marine Institute

CAUTIONS: algae-coated boulders and cobbles are very slippery; cliffs are unstable; tidepools become more isolated farther north

FACILITIES: small picnic area near Marine Institute

Locality OC-20
Doheny State Beach (See Map 40)

The Visitor's Center has a small gift shop, as well as several aquarium tanks where you can see many of the life forms inhabiting our coastal waters. A simulated tidepool inside the center has various sea stars, California mussels and leaf barnacles (which had their "feet" extended for feeding when I was there). The beach park is generally crowded but has a small cobbly area where you can observe some tidepool plants and animals. But you won't be able to see the diversity and abundance characteristic of our tidepools, partly because of thoughtless collecting. When I was there, dozens of people were collecting tidepool animals in buckets, and the stench from rotting snails, crabs and sea hares was a sad indicator of the hundreds of creatures dying that day. I hope collecting at these beaches soon will be better regulated, either legally or by our own sensitivity. The nearby jetties are in many ways more interesting because they harbor a greater variety of life. Leaf barnacles (you may see them feeding), mussels and other tidepool organisms are common on the rocks.

RATING: less than 1

NATURE OF ROCKS: cobbles

PRESENT BUT NOT ABUNDANT: small acorn barnacles, limpets, a variety of snails, hermit crabs, sargasso weed, California sea hares, leaf barnacles, California mussels

PARKING/FEES: adequate parking in lots with fee to enter state beach; generally crowded

ACCESS: easy walk from parking lot over sandy beach

CAUTIONS: cobbles are slippery

FACILITIES: restrooms, showers, drinking fountains, snack bar, lifeguard services, gift shop at Visitor's Center

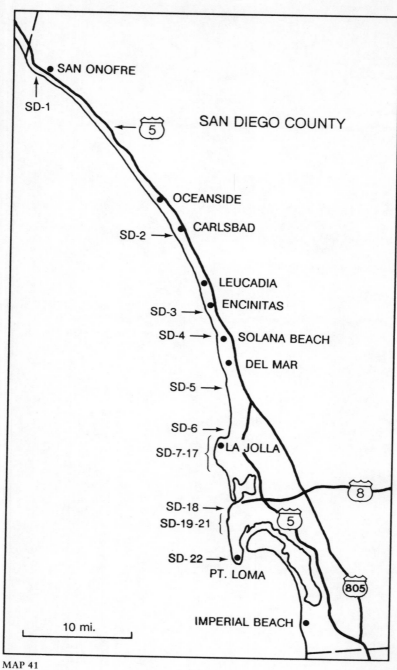

SAN ONOFRE

SD-1

SAN DIEGO COUNTY

5

OCEANSIDE

SD-2 → CARLSBAD

LEUCADIA

SD-3 → ENCINITAS

SD-4 → SOLANA BEACH

DEL MAR

SD-5 →

SD-6 →

SD-7-17 { • LA JOLLA

8

SD-18 →

SD-19-21 {

5

SD-22 →

PT. LOMA

805

10 mi.

IMPERIAL BEACH

MAP 41

San Diego County

Although San Diego County (see Map 41) offers some spectacular tidepools, most are located in the La Jolla vicinity, a rocky headland renowned for its breathtaking vistas of crashing waves and rocky cliffs.

SAN ONOFRE TO DEL MAR

[Northern San Diego County has few tidepools since the coastal area is predominantly sandy beaches. The few pools here are generally small but accessibility is easy and involves only a short walk. The ratings are low due to size and limited diversity. However, they are fully enjoyable.]

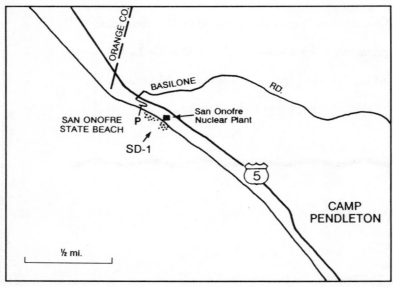

MAP 42

Locality SD-1
San Onofre State Beach (See Map 42)

Here tidepools consist of two cobbly areas interspersed with sandy pools. You'll need a low tide to see these tidepools. Sand castle worms are abundant, especially on the tops of the rocks. Be careful not to step on them. The park, with its lawn and picnic tables, is popular with surfers and tidepool explorers alike.

RATING: 1

NATURE OF ROCKS: cobbles

ESPECIALLY ABUNDANT: acorn barnacles, California sea hares,

tegula snails, hermit crabs, various limpets, giant green anemones, coralline red algae, sargasso weed, sand castle worms, scaly tube snails, chitons, striped sea slugs, surfgrass

OF SPECIAL INTEREST: beautiful masses of sand castle worms

PARKING/FEES: large parking lot; fee

ACCESS: park exit is along Basilone Rd. about 1 mile south of the freeway exit from I-5; to park follow signs indicating beach access; tidepools are a short walk from the parking lot

CAUTIONS: cobbles can be slippery

FACILITIES: restrooms, drinking fountains, lifeguards, picnic tables in park

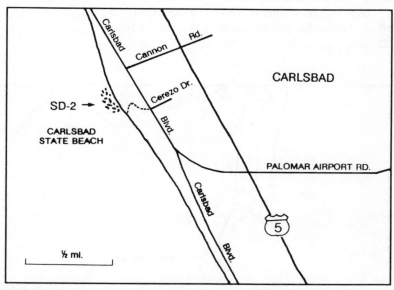

MAP 43

Locality SD-2
Carlsbad State Beach (See Map 43)

This small tidepool area lies just north of the intersection of Palomar Airport Rd. and Carlsbad Boulevard. The easiest way to find it is by parking along Carlsbad Boulevard near the corner of Cerezo Drive. If you walk toward the cliffs you will see a rocky area to the north extending from a small point. A path on the north side of a chain link fence leads to the beach. Because it is so small, even a few people can make it feel crowded. It is best visited when the tides are negative, if possible. However, there is much to see here, especially the purple olives abounding in the sandy areas of the isolated pools.

RATING: 1

NATURE OF ROCKS: low rock benches

ESPECIALLY ABUNDANT: purple olive snails, giant green anemones, coralline red algae, sand castle worms, scaly tube snails, mussels, wavy turbans, chitons, surfgrass, southern sea palm

PARKING/FEES: parking along the west side of Carlsbad Blvd.; no fees

ACCESS: dirt pathway located on the north side of a chain link fence near the corner of Cerezo Dr. and Carlsbad Blvd.

CAUTIONS: dirt pathway is steep toward the base

FACILITIES: none

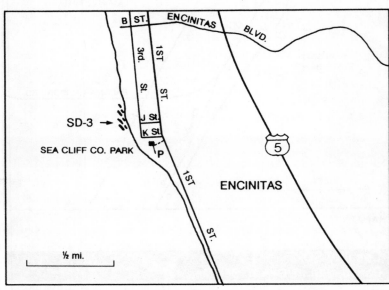

MAP 44

Locality SD-3
Sea Cliff County Park (See Map 44)

This roadside park is just south of K Street in Encinitas. Flat table-like rocks dip gently to the north, providing a small but beautiful tidepool area. California mussels, leaf barnacles, scaly tube snails and purple olives are the predominant organisms. Most interesting are the spectacular masses of sand castle worms coating so many rocks here. Another interesting feature is the distinctive olive-green rock composing the pools. It has an unusual color and is full of embedded shells from a old fossil oyster reef 45-50 million years old. Sea Cliff County Park is a favorite picnic spot that may be crowded, especially in the summer months.

RATING: 2

NATURE OF ROCKS: flat, table-like rock layers

ESPECIALLY ABUNDANT: California mussels, leaf barnacles, sand castle worms, scaly tube snails, purple olives, sea anemones, chitons, acorn barnacles, striped shore crabs, coralline red algae

OF SPECIAL INTEREST: spectacular masses of sand castle worms; fossil oyster reef preserved in the rock layers

PARKING/FEES: parking lot; no fees

ACCESS: long stairway leads to beach from parking lot; tidepools are north of stairway

CAUTIONS: none

FACILITIES: public restrooms, shower, drinking fountain

Locality SD-4
Cardiff State Beach (See Map 45)

Just off Pacific Coast Highway north of Lomas Santa Fe Dr. lies Cardiff State Beach. You will need a low tide, preferably negative, to see the diversity of life in these tidepools. The same fossil oyster reef rock seen at Sea Cliff County Park (SD-3), is also present here, but is partially obscured by barnacles, mussels, and large sand castle worm masses. For a rewarding look at life in the lower intertidal zone, you must be willing to wade through some water. In the seaward section you can find some of the largest acorn barnacles found in San Diego County. Sponges, purple olives and scaly tube snails are also common. At the southern end is a more diverse habitat with crevices, cobbles and isolated pools. California sea hares, hermit crabs and abundant aggregating sea anemones make this area their home.

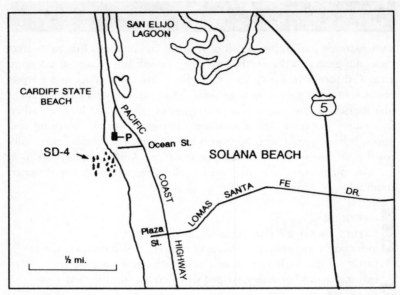

MAP 45

RATING: 2

NATURE OF ROCKS: flat, table-like rock benches

ESPECIALLY ABUNDANT: barnacles, mussels, aggregating sea anemones, coralline red algae, sand castle worms, giant green sea anemones, acorn barnacles, sponges, purple olives, scaly tube snails, California sea hares, hermit crabs

OF SPECIAL INTEREST: very large acorn barnacles; fossil oyster reef preserved in rock layers

PARKING/FEES: large parking lot; no fees

ACCESS: short walk south from parking lot

CAUTIONS: none

FACILITIES: lifeguard services, portable bathrooms

Locality SD-5a, b
Torrey Pines State Beach (See Map 46)

To access these tidepools either walk south from Torrey Pines State Beach, or take the "Beach Trail" from Torrey Pines State Park for a fee. If you walk south from the Beach, be sure to explore the rock layers making up the cliffs. They represent ancient beach deposits. As you approach the first tidepool area, a greenish colored flat rock appears in the outcrops, part of the fossil oyster reef mentioned earlier.

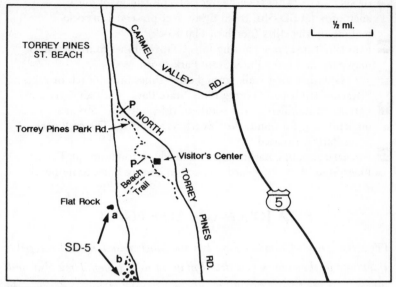

MAP 46

The first tidepool area is called Flat Rock (SD-5a). Depending on where you look on Flat Rock, you will find different plants and animals, revealing their particular ecological preferences. For example, on the north side of the rock, anemones and sand castle worms are abundant. The south side of the rock harbors masses of California mussels and leaf barnacles. If you venture to the top of Flat Rock, you will see periwinkles and limpets in the drier areas, with anemones, barnacles and mussels in the wetter regions. Spectacular clusters of sand castle worms and some large giant owl limpets cover the front face of the rock.

Better tidepools, consisting of large boulders which are somewhat difficult to get around, lie south of Flat Rock (SD-5b). Although it is a long walk from Flat Rock, it is worth the trip. Along with other abundant life, you will encounter some of the largest and greenest giant green anemones in the county. Some are 5-6 inches across. This is also a fine place for bird-watching.

RATING: 2-2½
NATURE OF ROCKS: rock benches, boulders and cobbles
ESPECIALLY ABUNDANT: giant green and aggregating anemones, sand castle worms, California mussels, leaf barnacles, periwinkles, limpets, acorn barnacles, giant owl limpets, chitons, southern sea palm, coralline red algae

OF SPECIAL INTEREST: very large and colorful giant green anemones (at SD-5b); fossil oyster reef preserved in rocks making up the cliffs (north of Flat Rock)

PARKING/FEES: large parking lot at Torrey Pines State Beach, or may park in Torrey Pines State Park (with fees)

ACCESS: either long walk from Torrey Pines State Beach or take "Beach Trail" from Torrey Pines State Park (with an entry fee)

CAUTIONS: boulders at the southern tidepools (SD-5b) are difficult to get around; the "Beach Trail" from Torrey Pines State Park is isolated

FACILITIES: public bathrooms and drinking fountains at Torrey Pines State Park; lifeguard services on Torrey Pines State Beach

LA JOLLA TO FALSE POINT

[This San Diego County region has the most abundant and accessible tidepools in the county (see detail map on next page). They also rank among the best due to rocky points and protected coves. Because the rocks extending from land are much thicker in this area, the tides don't have to be quite as low here as in other areas such as North County. Coastal views are spectacular. In general, the southern localities of La Jolla will be less crowded than the northern ones, resulting in easier parking.]

Locality SD-6
Dike Rock (North of Scripps Pier) (See Map 47)

This tidepool area is interesting for several reasons. First, the geology is unique. Most of the rocks in the coastal areas of Southern California represent ancient beach deposits and are largely sandstones and silt-stones. The layering is obvious in the cliffs facing the beach. These rocks are about 40 to 50 million years old. If you look carefully at the main rock bench extending out into the ocean, you'll see that it is not the same rock that makes up the cliffs. It is darker and harder, and looks similar to lava rock common on volcanic islands. This vertical outcrop was formed from hot, molten rock which forced its way up through the layered beach rocks of the cliffs about 10-12 million years ago. This geologic feature is called a dike, hence the name "Dike Rock," one of the most prominent features of these tidepools.

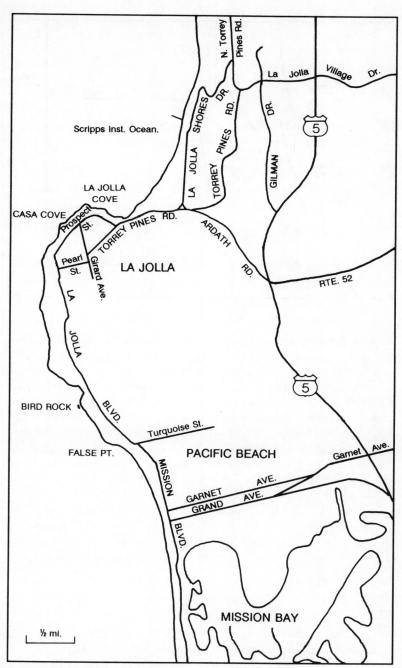

Detail of La Jolla to False Point.

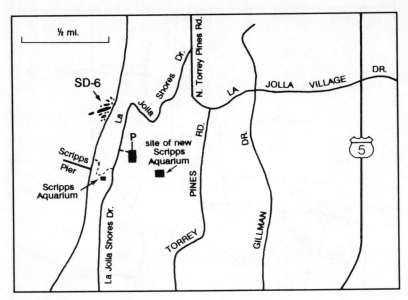

MAP 47

This tidepool area is enhanced by the nearby Scripps Aquarium-Museum, part of Scripps Institution of Oceanography. It exhibits marine life native to Southern California as well as from tropical regions such as Micronesia. The aquarium houses a small simulated tidepool in front where you can watch the behavior of some of the plants and animals found in tidepools around San Diego. Note that the aquarium will be moving in the near future. Its new site for the new aquarium is shown on Map 47.

Dike Rock is home to a wide variety of life forms making it one of the best tidepool areas in San Diego County. This spot has a few drawbacks, however. It can be crowded and more difficult to explore than others because of the large dike. Also, much of the area on the north side of the dike is submerged even during low tide. You can't see many of the interesting life forms here without getting your feet wet. Take care as rocks in the submerged pools are covered with slippery algae.

 RATING: 3

NATURE OF ROCKS: large rock bench, boulders and cobbles

ESPECIALLY ABUNDANT: giant green and aggregating sea anemones, California mussels, acorn and leaf barnacles, sponges, sand castle worms, scaly tube snails, surfgrass, southern sea palm, sea lettuce, spongeweed, California sea hares, limpets, hermit crabs, tegula snails

OF SPECIAL INTEREST: nearby Scripps Aquarium-Museum and Scripps Institution of Oceanography; geology buffs will find the large rock bench making up much of the tidepool area interesting because this is an "igneous intrusion" or "dike"

PARKING/FEES: along La Jolla Shores Drive (time limits indicated by signs are strictly enforced); aquarium visitors may park in a large visitor's lot on the east side of La Jolla Shores Blvd. (indicated by a sign)

ACCESS: enter beach by stairways south of Scripps Pier or by small access drive just north of the pier; tidepools are about 200 yds. north of the pier

CAUTIONS: rocks are difficult to traverse and slippery

FACILITIES: public restrooms at Scripps Aquarium-Museum

Locality SD-7
South of Marine Room (See Map 48)

This pleasant area is characterized by large, flat rock outcrops, easy to cross. If the tide is low enough (less than 0.5 ft.) you will be able to see much of the area without getting wet, but if you go south, you will probably have to wade through a shallow inlet or two. This area is more isolated with a small sandy cove where you can enjoy a picnic. It

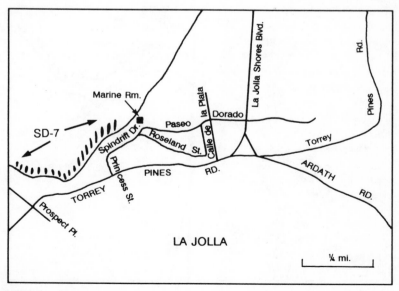

MAP 48

is seldom crowded at these tidepools, and because they are large, you can see a lot without encountering others. As a result, the tidepool life hasn't been trampled as much as at other La Jolla pools, leaving a wide variety of life to behold. Sculpted masses of scaly tube snails and sand castle worms are especially interesting. Bring your bird-watching glasses too.

RATING: 4

NATURE OF ROCKS: flat, table-like rock outcrops with intermittent shallow-water channels

ESPECIALLY ABUNDANT: sand castle worms, scaly tube snails, wavy turbans, tegula snails, hermit crabs, sea anemones, spongeweed, surfgrass, sargasso weed

OF SPECIAL INTEREST: beautiful scaly tube snails and sand castle worms

PARKING/FEES: parking on nearby streets; no fees

ACCESS: coastal entrance near the Marine Room Restaurant at the corner of Roseland St. and Spindrift Dr.; tidepools are to the south

CAUTIONS: rocks can be slippery; be sure you have a low negative tide; you will probably get wet

FACILITIES: none

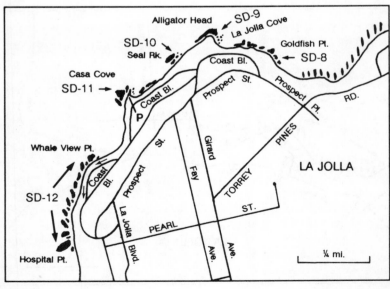

MAP 49

Locality SD-8
Goldfish Point (See Map 49)

Goldfish Point is named for the abundance of bright orange Garibaldi fish in the area. Don't let the low rating discourage you. This rating derives from the steep pathway to the tidepools and the smallness of the tidepool area. You must also be sure the tide is very low: a negative tide is best. Plants and animals are abundant. Of particular interest are the thousands of troglodyte chitons in oval-shaped depressions in the soft sandstone. This is also an excellent area for snorkeling.

RATING: 1½

NATURE OF ROCKS: steep cliffs and flat rock outcrops

ESPECIALLY ABUNDANT: aggregating and giant green anemones, chitons, leaf barnacles, limpets

OF SPECIAL INTEREST: troglodyte chitons burrowed in the soft sandstone

PARKING/FEES: street parking is available along Coast Blvd. but is scarce due to the popularity of the area; parking is easier in early morning; nearby parking lots are available for a parking fee

ACCESS: very steep dirt pathway leading from the cliffs near the La Jolla Cave and Shell Shop on the north end of Coast Blvd.

CAUTIONS: pathway is very steep; be sure the tide is very low

FACILITIES: none

Locality SD-9
La Jolla Cove/Alligator Head (See Map 49)

It is best to visit these tidepools during low tides. Incoming waves hit the point forcefully so be prepared to get splashed. At La Jolla Cove, the mid-sized boulders can be slippery due to algae. Animals typical of a cobbly area are abundant. On some of the rock outcrops you will notice thousands of oval-shaped depressions harboring troglodyte chitons. Farther south on Alligator Head, other plants and animals abound. You might even spy a lobster lurking in one of the shady pools.

These tidepools are popular because of their proximity to downtown La Jolla and the beach at La Jolla Cove. Thus you can shop, swim, snorkel and explore tidepools in one outing. La Jolla Cove boasts a protected underwater park. Parking is available along the street but is difficult to come by, particularly in the summer when it can be very crowded.

RATING: 3

NATURE OF ROCKS: large rock benches, boulders and cobbles

ESPECIALLY ABUNDANT: hermit crabs, chitons, tegula snails, sand castle worms, scaly tube snails, leaf barnacles, sea anemones, California mussels, surfgrass, California spiny lobsters, coralline red algae

OF SPECIAL INTEREST: thousands of troglodyte chitons in the soft sandstone

PARKING/FEES: street parking along Coast Blvd. is limited due to the popularity of the area; early morning is a better time to find parking; nearby parking lots are available for a parking fee

ACCESS: either take the stairway down to the cove to get to the north end of Alligator Head or access from the walkway along Alligator Head to see the flatter rock outcrops

CAUTIONS: beware of strong surf at the seaward faces of the rocks; cobbles and boulders may be slippery

FACILITIES: adjacent Ellen Browning Scripps Park provides public restrooms, showers, drinking fountain, and lifeguard services

Locality SD-10
Shell Beach (See Map 49)

This area is adjacent to Seal Rock, and is a great place to view seals sunning on the rocks. The best time to see them is in the early morning. You'll have to look carefully because they blend with the rocks. Once you notice one seal, the others will become apparent. I have seen as many as 15 basking lazily in the morning sun. Tidepool life abounds here as well. Shell Beach is also a fine place for a picnic.

RATING: 2

NATURE OF ROCKS: cobbles and boulders

ESPECIALLY ABUNDANT: rockweed, sea lettuce, coralline red algae, tegula snails, wavy turbans

OF SPECIAL INTEREST: seals on large rock off beach

PARKING/FEES: along Coast Blvd. and nearby streets; get there early to avoid crowds

ACCESS: stairway just north of Shell Beach leads to beach and tidepools

CAUTIONS: cobbles are slippery

FACILITIES: none

Locality SD-11
Casa Cove ("Children's Pool") (See Map 49)

The cove is a protected beach area. Tidepools inside the cove are small but contain a variety of life. Sometimes you can find the egg masses of sea hares washed up on the beach (see Plate 30b) even if you aren't lucky enough to spot the sea hares themselves. South of the breakwater lies a larger tidepool area with more variety than inside the cove. You'll probably need to wade through some pools to get to some of the better spots, but BE SURE YOU DO THIS ONLY AT LOW TIDE AND LOW SURF. Incoming waves hitting the breakwater can be very powerful and dangerous even during moderate tides. One of the obvious features in the flat rocks are the deep round holes which create luminous, protected pools filled with all types of plants and animals. These holes result from large round boulders and cobbles which have weathered out from the rocks, leaving circular depressions which fill with water. Many of these pools are ideal for photography. Farther south exists a small, rocky point with additional tidepools. It offers the same life forms typical of the Casa Cove area, but is less crowded.

RATING: 2½

NATURE OF ROCKS: rock benches, boulders and cobbles

ESPECIALLY ABUNDANT: keyhole and false limpets, barnacles, sea anemones, sea hares, tegula snails, coralline red algae, sargasso weed

PARKING/FEES: small parking lot and parking on nearby streets; no fees

ACCESS: stairway to cove and to tidepools south of cove

CAUTIONS: strong surf hits the breakwater and rocks with force

FACILITIES: public restrooms, drinking fountains, showers, lifeguard services

Locality SD-12
Whale View Point to Hospital Point (See Map 49)

Names for this area are derived from the obvious: Whale View Point is an excellent locality to view gray whales on their annual migration during the winter from November to March, and Hospital Point is adjacent to the large La Jolla Medical Clinic complex. The tidepools are extensive with flat rock outcroppings sloping gently toward the sea. You need not get wet to see a good variety of life forms, and the walk is easy. Sandy beaches encompass the area and are ideal for a picnic.

RATING: 4

NATURE OF ROCKS: flat, table-like rock benches

ESPECIALLY ABUNDANT: acorn barnacles, leaf barnacles, California mussels, striped shore crabs, hermit crabs, sea anemones, periwinkles, sea lettuce, feather boa kelp, variety of limpets, chitons

PARKING/FEES: parking on nearby streets; no fees

ACCESS: enter along Coast Blvd. or from the beaches north and south of the tidepools

CAUTIONS: beware of strong surf at seaward edges of rock benches

FACILITIES: lifeguard services on nearby beaches

Locality SD-13
Rockpile and Little Point (See Map 50)

Rockpile and Little Point are two distinct tidepool areas. The northern tidepools are called Rockpile, a name descriptive of its many boulders. Here you will encounter some of the largest chitons in San Diego County. Many are 3 inches long with a "mossy" fringe or girdle around their edges. The rocks and chitons are covered with slippery

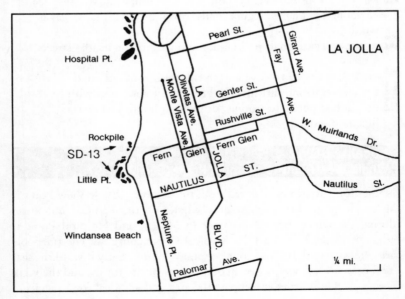

MAP 50

algae. Farther south is another set of tidepools at Little Point. Although the rocks are flat, many are quite slippery. Small, deep pools in the flat rocks harbor sea anemones that are fully opened, exposing their rich, green tentacles. You'll need a low negative tide to visit both of these areas.

RATING: 2½

NATURE OF ROCKS: rock benches and boulders

ESPECIALLY ABUNDANT: aggregating and giant green anemones, chitons, volcano barnacles, leaf barnacles, California mussels, coralline algae, feather boa kelp, sargasso weed, surfgrass

OF SPECIAL INTEREST: very large chitons

PARKING/FEES: parking on nearby streets; no fees

ACCESS: walkway at the corner of Fern Glen and Neptune Place or walk from beaches to the south or north

CAUTIONS: rocks are very slippery

FACILITIES: none

Locality SD-14
Big Rock Point (See Map 51)

Gently sloping flat rocks make this an easy tidepool to navigate, although the tide must be very low (0.0 ft. or negative) if you access the

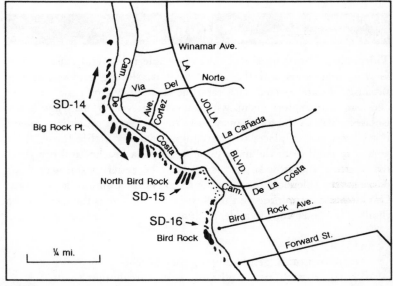

MAP 51

area from Windansea Beach to the north. The organisms are relatively undisturbed by humans, and some massive sand castle worm structures appear in the low intertidal zone. Soft sandstones, also in the low intertidal, contain thousands of chitons. You will find some spectacular giant green anemones, some reaching 6 inches across. Although the rocks are easy and safe to traverse, be careful of the strong surf at the seaward edge. Intermittent sandy coves provide ideal picnic areas.

RATING: 4

NATURE OF ROCKS: gently sloping rock benches

ESPECIALLY ABUNDANT: California mussels, leaf barnacles, variety of limpets, acorn barnacles, periwinkles, chitons, scaly tube snails, tegula snails, volcano barnacles, sargasso weed, coralline red algae, giant keyhole limpets, aggregating and giant green anemones, rockweed, striped shore crabs, sand castle worms

OF SPECIAL INTEREST: very nice sand castle worms; thousands of troglodyte chitons; very large giant green anemones

PARKING/FEES: parking along nearby streets; no fees

ACCESS: walk south from Windansea Beach to the north; or enter from Camino de la Costa between Cortez Place and Via del Norte

CAUTIONS: strong surf at the seaward faces of the rocks

FACILITIES: none

Locality SD-15
North Bird Rock (See Map 51)

Tidepools at North Bird Rock are enjoyable for several reasons. The view is marvelous and the rocks are flat, sloping gently seaward. Because they are covered with coralline algae, they aren't too slippery, and you can explore them without getting wet. It also has many isolated pools in the rocks away from the surf zone, providing camera buffs with perfect places to photograph a variety of life forms. This area is isolated from the more popular La Jolla beaches and is a good retreat from the crowds. Access couldn't be easier; a stairway leads down to the tidepools from the southern end of Camino de la Costa. One of the most impressive things to catch your eye is the spectacle of thousands of inch-long oval depressions in the rocks harboring chitons.

RATING: 3

NATURE OF ROCKS: gently dipping rock benches

ESPECIALLY ABUNDANT: sand castle worms, scaly tube snails,

periwinkles, coralline algae, chitons, surfgrass, sargasso weed, feather boa kelp, spongeweed, rockweed, striped shore crabs, tegula snails, hermit crabs, leaf barnacles, acorn barnacles, California mussels

OF SPECIAL INTEREST: thousands of troglodyte chitons in the sandstone

PARKING/FEES: street parking in the nearby neighborhood; no fees

ACCESS: stairway leading down to the tidepools from small parking area at the end of Camino de la Costa Blvd.

CAUTIONS: none

FACILITIES: none

Locality SD-16
Bird Rock (See Map 51)

"Bird Rock" derives its name from the large, bird-inhabited rock predominating these tidepools making it a bird-watcher's paradise. Among a variety of birds, snowy egrets are one of the most common. The rock itself provides an interesting feature for understanding the various physical zonations found in tidepools. On this single rock organisms range from high to middle intertidal varieties. The top half is a tan to olive colored sandstone. Because it is exposed to air during periods of low tide, this portion of the rock is covered with limpets and periwinkles. The lower half of the rock is a soft sandstone. The pink coloration comes from pink encrusting coralline algae coating its surface. Thousands of chitons have burrowed depressions into this rock. Sea anemones crowd the base, indicating a lower intertidal zone submerged most of the time. The Bird Rock area is diverse, peppered with flat rocks interspersed with cobbles and boulders. The plants and animals are similarly diverse. This is one of the few tidepools in San Diego County still housing an abundance of sea stars, sea cucumbers and sea urchins. PLEASE DON'T DISTURB THEM so that we can continue to enjoy their presence here. It is best to visit during a fairly low tide.

RATING: 4

NATURE OF ROCKS: flat rock benches, boulders and cobbles

ESPECIALLY ABUNDANT: limpets, periwinkles, tegula snails, hermit crabs, aggregating anemones, giant green anemones, sea urchins, scaly tube snails, coralline red algae, chitons, sea stars, pink encrusting coralline algae, striped shore crabs, wavy turbans, rockweed, sponge weed, sargasso weed, surfgrass, feather boa kelp

OF SPECIAL INTEREST: thousands of troglodyte chitons; sea stars, sea cucumbers and sea urchins are commonly found here

PARKING/FEES: street parking along Bird Rock Ave.; no fees

ACCESS: a partial stairway at the end of Bird Rock Ave. leads to a set of large boulders; climbing down them may be difficult

CAUTIONS: must climb over large boulders to access tidepools; many of the rocks in the tidepools are slippery

FACILITIES: none

Locality SD-17
False Point (See Map 52)

I always feel a bit guilty when I visit False Point. So many snails and hermit crabs abound that it is impossible not to crush some of them. This tidepool is characterized by cobbles weathered out from the cliff rocks. Plants and animals typical of cobbly tidepools flourish here. California sea hares are abundant but blend remarkably well with the cobbles, so be especially careful not to trample these defenseless creatures. The plentiful rockweed covering many of the rocks makes footing precarious. Only visit if you are prepared to walk a fair distance over slippery cobbles. If you keep moving north about 100 yds., the tidepool area flattens out and is less cobbly.

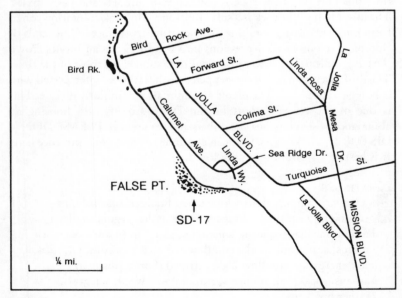

MAP 52

RATING: 2½

NATURE OF ROCKS: cobbles, boulders and rock benches

ESPECIALLY ABUNDANT: tegula snails, hermit crabs, California sea hares, striped shore crabs, acorn barnacles, giant keyhole limpets, bat stars, brittle stars, giant green anemones, California mussels, leaf barnacles, rockweed, sargasso weed, feather boa kelp, coralline red algae

PARKING/FEES: parking along nearby streets; no fees

ACCESS: a stairway at the corner of Sea Ridge Dr. and Linda Way leads down to the cobbly beach area; the tidepools are north of this stairway

CAUTIONS: cobbles are very slippery

FACILITIES: none

OCEAN BEACH TO POINT LOMA

[Here you may find a wide variety of tidepool habitats due to differing rock outcrops and some of the most variation in tidepool habitats in San Diego County (see detail map on next page). Rough sandstones typical of the La Jolla tidepools characterize Ocean Beach to Sunset Cliffs. Eventually these grade into more slippery claystones at the southern end of Sunset Cliffs and Point Loma. Also rocky points with rough surf are close to a large coastal embayment where the waters are more quiet. These variations make tidepooling interesting and rewarding.]

Locality SD-18
Ocean Beach Pier to Cable St. (See Map 53)

Tidepools from Ocean Beach Pier to Cable St. are extensive, containing a wide variety of life forms. Near the pier, the tidepools are more disturbed by the number of visitors they receive. I have given these a rating of "1". As you progress south, however, the tidepool habitats change and contain much more abundant and diverse life. I have rated these "3½." Intermittent boulders and beach areas create several breaks in the tidepools. All accesses have a stairway leading to the beach or tidepool area, except for the Cable St. access. This one deadends and becomes a paved roadway leading to a cobbly area to be crossed carefully before reaching the flat tidepool area.

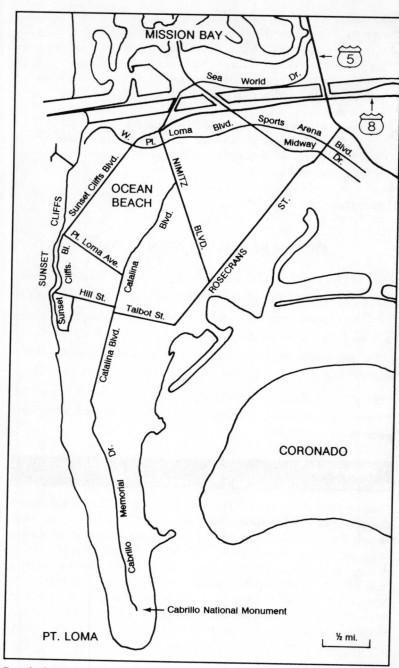

Detail of Ocean Beach to Point Loma.

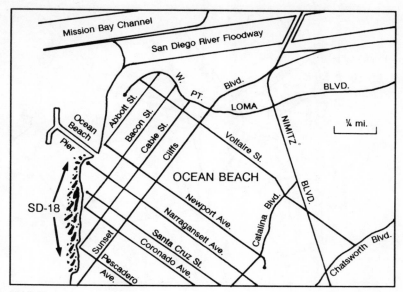

MAP 53

 RATING: 1-3½

NATURE OF ROCKS: flat rock benches, boulders and cobbles

ESPECIALLY ABUNDANT: volcano barnacles, tegula snails, hermit crabs, chitons, limpets, periwinkles, acorn barnacles, California mussels, leaf barnacles, coralline red algae, southern sea palm, surfgrass, sargasso weed, feather boa kelp, giant green and aggregating anemones, sand castle worms

 OF SPECIAL INTEREST: thousands of troglodyte chitons

PARKING/FEES: parking along nearby streets; no fees

ACCESS: several accesses: walk from Ocean Beach Pier; stairway at the end of Santa Cruz St.; paved entrance at the end of Cable St.

CAUTIONS: rocks can be slippery; beware of strong surf at the seaward faces of the rocks; access at Cable St. is very cobbly and difficult to traverse

FACILITIES: restrooms, showers and drinking fountains in Ocean Beach area

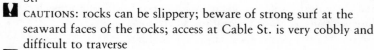

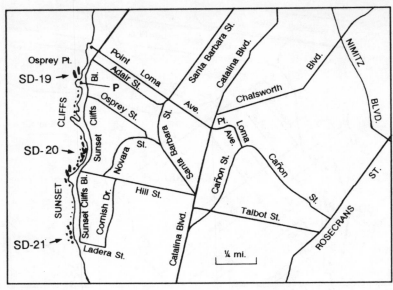

MAP 54

Locality SD-19
Osprey Point (See Map 54)

Two rock benches extend seaward to produce Osprey Point tidepools.
Although the rocks are flat, they become slippery in places, and surf can
be quite powerful at the seaward edge.

RATING: 1½

NATURE OF ROCKS: Gently dipping rock benches

ESPECIALLY ABUNDANT: periwinkles, acorn barnacles, various
limpets, striped shore crabs, giant green and aggregating
anemones, hermit crabs, surfgrass, feather boa kelp, coralline
red algae, leaf barnacles, giant owl limpets, California mussels,
large chitons, encrusting coralline algae

OF SPECIAL INTEREST: thousands of troglodyte chitons burrowed
in soft sandstone

PARKING/FEES: two small parking lots along Sunset Cliffs Blvd.
between Adair St. and Osprey St.; no fees

ACCESS: short pathways down from parking lots

CAUTIONS: slippery rocks; strong surf hits point

FACILITIES: none

Locality SD-20
Sunset Cliffs at Hill St. (See Map 54)

Within this large coastal embayment, flat rocks with intermittent crevices and pools make up the tidepools. Because wave action is low, this is an excellent area to observe lower intertidal life forms. Two steep pathways lead down to the area; one at the end of Hill St. and one just north of Hill St. This latter entrance is preferable, although large boulders at the base of each are difficult to traverse.

RATING: 3

NATURE OF ROCKS: flat, low rock benches with intermittent crevices

ESPECIALLY ABUNDANT: tegula snails, hermit crabs, sea lettuce, limpets, large chitons, aggregating anemones, giant green anemones, sargasso weed, coralline red algae, surfgrass, striped shore crabs, volcano barnacles, sea stars, feather boa kelp

PARKING/FEES: along Sunset Cliffs Blvd. or nearby streets; no fees

ACCESS: steep pathways: one at end of Hill St. and the preferred path just north of Hill St.

CAUTIONS: pathways are very steep and there are boulders at the base to cross

FACILITIES: none

Locality SD-21
Sunset Cliffs at Ladera St. (See Map 54)

A long stairway at the southern end of Sunset Cliffs on the corner of Sunset Cliffs Blvd. and Ladera St. leads down to boulders and cobbles, and eventually to flatter, slippery claystone rocks. Beach areas extend to the south.

RATING: 1

NATURE OF ROCKS: boulders, cobbles and slippery claystones

ESPECIALLY ABUNDANT: acorn barnacles, limpets, volcano barnacles, chitons, giant green and aggregating anemones, leaf barnacles, coralline red algae, periwinkles

OF SPECIAL INTEREST: thousands of troglodyte chitons in soft sandstone

PARKING/FEES: parking along Sunset Cliffs Blvd. and nearby streets; no fees

ACCESS: long stairway at corner of Sunset Cliffs Blvd. and Ladera St.

CAUTIONS: rocks are very slippery

FACILITIES: none

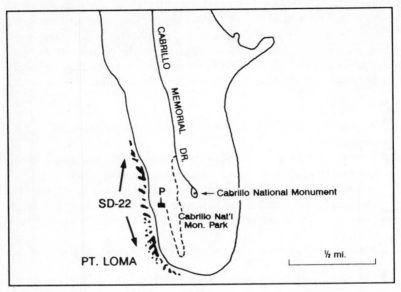

MAP 55

Locality SD-22
Point Loma/Cabrillo National Monument Park (See Map 55)

Point Loma is characterized by relatively soft, fairly slippery claystone rock. Most of the tidepool creatures inhabit the cracks and crevices. This is a popular spot for tidepooling in San Diego county, and has been set aside as a natural preserve in the Cabrillo National Monument Park. Signs near the path to the tidepools provide information about the common plants and animals found here. The tidepools are easily accessible with ample parking nearby. Although a visit to the Monument costs a small fee, a visit to the tidepools is free. Be sure to take the right-hand turnoff before the park entrance. Cabrillo National Monument Park, however, sponsors nature walks to the tidepools and offers a slide presentation called "Steps to the Sea," providing information on our local tidepools.

RATING: 3½

NATURE OF ROCKS: rock benches, boulders and cobbles

ESPECIALLY ABUNDANT: limpets, periwinkles, leaf barnacles,

California mussels, giant green anemones, aggregating anemones, rockweed, coralline red algae, spongeweed, tegula snails, hermit crabs, California sea hares, surfgrass, southern sea palm, sand castle worms, sponges

PARKING/FEES: free parking in large lot at tidepool area; fee to enter Cabrillo National Monument Park

ACCESS: long but easy dirt pathway leading from large parking lot

CAUTIONS: rock benches are claystone and very slippery; cobbles are also slippery

FACILITIES: none at tidepool area; Cabrillo National Monument Park provides public restrooms, drinking fountains, telephones, and gift shop

Plant
Life

O ceanic plant life ranges from microscopic phytoplankton to large seaweeds which may be hundreds of feet long. Phytoplankton is the abundant food source for many tidepool animals. Although phytoplankton exists in large numbers, it is tiny and invisible to the naked eye. What we can see are the non-microscopic plants. A detailed description of each plant is given below. The common name is given first and the scientific names are italicized in parentheses.

Plate 1. COMMON SURFGRASS *(Phyllospadix scouleri)*
This slender, vivid green "grass" has long, flat blades. It grows in large clumps or beds exposed during low tide and submerged at high tide. It is found attached to rocks in the middle to low intertidal zones to a depth of about 40-50 ft. Surfgrass is particularly beautiful as it waves back and forth in the waves.

Plate 2. SPONGEWEED *(Codium fragile)*
The cylindrical fronds of this dark green alga have a spongy texture and form heavy, drooping clumps on rocks, resulting in its nickname "Dead Man's Fingers." It is common in the high to low intertidal zones.

Plate 3. SEA LETTUCE *(Ulva californica)*
Sea Lettuce commonly forms a bright green, leafy coating on rocks in the high to low intertidal zones. Individual leaves of this seaweed are usually an inch to several inches long and may have ruffled edges.

Plate 4. SEA BUBBLE *(Colpomenia sinuosa)*
This smooth, bubble-shaped alga is common in the middle intertidal zone. The hollow "bubbles" average ½-3 inches across and are initially greenish brown, becoming progressively browner with age.

Plate 5. SARGASSO WEED *(Sargassum agardhianum)*
Clumps of Sargasso Weed are common in the middle and low intertidal zones, and frequently occur in isolated pools among the rocks, particularly during the winter months. The fine strands of this alga are dark brown and can grow to 4 feet long. The strands are covered with

tiny, bead-like spheres filled with gas which give the leaves buoyancy so they are always near the water's surface where sunlight is the brightest. This seaweed is abundant in the Sargasso Sea of the Atlantic Ocean.

Plate 6. ROCKWEED *(Pelvetia fastigiata)*
This greenish brown alga is one of the most common plants in the tidepools of southern California. Its slender, branching, 8-10 inch long fronds cover many of the rocks in a thick, shag carpet. Rockweed is particularly dense in the middle and low intertidal zones.

KELP

[Kelp is common off California's coastline. It prefers these cold waters and rocky sea floors to grip with its strong root-like "holdfast." Kelp beds provide an ideal, protected environment for invertebrates and fish. A dive through a kelp forest is unforgettable—not only because of the abundance of life, but because spectacular views of sunlight filter through the kelp canopy on the water's surface. You may see large kelp beds from tidepools and beach areas of southern California. Although the larger species of kelp are limited to deeper waters, two smaller species of kelp (Southern Sea Palm and Feather Boa Kelp) *are common in the intertidal.]*

Plate 7. SOUTHERN SEA PALM *(Eisenia arborea)*
This small kelp averages 6 in. to 2 ft. in the middle and low intertidal zones, while in deeper waters it can reach heights of 4 feet or more. Southern Sea Palm has a short, rootlike holdfast and an erect stalk with 2 leafy fronds extending from the top. Unlike Rockweed which droops onto the rocks when exposed, the Southern Sea Palm stands erect on its sturdy stalk. Growth rings in the stalks of many sea palms indicate an age of 75 years or more.

Plate 8. FEATHER BOA KELP *(Egregia menziesii)*
This feathery-looking kelp is named for its fine, dark brown blades interspersed with larger, flatter blades. Like all kelp, Feather Boa Kelp attaches to rocks with a root-like "holdfast," and has small flotation bulbs allowing the long stalks to reach the surface where sunlight is the brightest. Feather Boa Kelp is common in the low intertidal zone, where it grows from one to several feet long, and in the subtidal zone, where it can reach lengths of up to 30 ft.

Plate 9. CORALLINE RED ALGAE *(Corallina vancouveriensis)*
The small, branching fronds of this alga are common and abundant in the low to middle intertidal tidepool zones. Live Coralline Red Algae appear pale to bright pink while dead coralline algae may be bleached

nearly white from the sun. This alga secretes lime, the same substance composing coral reefs. This makes for brittle, delicate fronds from 2-5 inches long. It can be found attached to shells of invertebrates. Commonly, a tuft of Coralline Red Algae will grow on top of a wavy turban shell.

Plate 10. PINK ENCRUSTING CORALLINE ALGAE
(Pseudolithophyllum spp. or Lithothamnion spp.)

This alga forms coats on rocks and invertebrate shells, painting them pink. Both species secrete lime crusts about 1 mm thick *(about 1/25 of an inch)* and are usually pink, although they may range from white to purple. The difference between the two species is the nature of their surfaces. *Pseudolithophyllum spp.* has numerous small bumps covering its surface, whereas *Lithothamnion spp.* is relatively smooth.

Animal
Life

M any animals inhabiting tidepools, such as fish, have a back-
bone or inner skeleton which supports their soft tissues.
They are called vertebrates. Most of the animals found in
tidepools, however, are invertebrates and lack an inner skeleton. Their
soft tissues are generally supported by an outer skeleton such as a shell.
Thus, the outer shell of the clam and the snail serve the same supportive
function as the vertebrate's internal skeleton. This outer shell also
provides the invertebrate with protection against predators and keeps it
from drying out when exposed to air. Some invertebrates, however,
such as the octopus and sea hare, lack a shell and are very susceptible to
predation. The octopus can move quickly to escape predators but the
sea hare moves so slowly that it might seem surprising that these
animals haven't become extinct. But the sea hare has an interesting
adaptation to prevent this—it lays eggs so profusely that the species is
assured to survive. There are records of individual sea hares laying as
many as 500 million eggs in just a few month's time.

Invertebrates have different adaptations for living in the various
habitats found in tidepools. For example, some worms burrow into the
sand where they feed on organic particles among the sand grains. But
most of the animals associated with tidepools live on the rocks where
some crawl slowly as they graze on algae while others attach firmly as
they filter the sea water for microscopic plankton (plants and animals
that are suspended in water). Nearly all of these tidepool invertebrates
began life as plankton themselves when they were in a larval stage.
These larvae eventually attached to rocks and changed their appearance
quite a bit to become the familiar life forms we see such as barnacles,
mussels and sea anemones.

Several major groups of invertebrates are common in the tidepools
of Southern California. Each is discussed separately in the order of
increasing complexity. The last organism described in this chapter is
not an invertebrate but instead is a primitive relative of vertebrates
called a "tunicate." As in the plant section, the common name is given
first, followed by the scientific name in parentheses.

SPONGES

[Pores are one of the distinguishing features of this group of animals. Water enters the sponge through these pores and eventually exits through one or more larger openings. During this process, the sponge filters food particles from the water. The skeletal support of sponges consists of either a fibrous material called "spongin" or microscopic needles called "spicules". Sponges are not as readily seen as other organisms in the tidepools, partly because they prefer the low intertidal zone where water is always present, but also because they are difficult to recognize by someone not familiar with them. One of the best ways to spot them is by looking for bright splashes of color such as red, orange and yellow. Colonies of sponges are typically a few inches to 2 feet across.]

Plate 11. VELVETY RED SPONGE *(Ophlitaspongia pennata)*
This brightly colored sponge forms a flat layer on the sides and bottoms of rocks in the middle and low intertidal zones. It is easily recognized as a bright splash of red to orange color.

SEA ANEMONES

[The sea anemones are part of a larger group that also includes corals and jellyfish. All members of this group have tentacles armed with stinging cells used to paralyze prey. In some members, such as the jellyfish and Man-O'-War, these stinging cells are quite potent and can even sting humans and large fish. Although the sea anemones found in Southern California's tidepools also have stinging cells in their tentacles, they are not potent enough to sting us. Instead, the tentacles feel slightly sticky to the touch, resulting from the stinging "barbs" adhering to your finger. This minor stinging, however, is strong enough to paralyze smaller organisms such as plankton, crabs or small fish, which make up the food of the sea anemone. Sea anemones obtain most of their food from wave activity which sweeps small food particles past (or against) the anemones' tentacles. Anemones also require well-oxygenated water. Thus, we find that anemones prefer areas where there is plenty of wave action.]

Plate 12. GIANT GREEN ANEMONE
    (Anthopleura xanthogrammica)
One of the most beautiful creatures in the tidepools is the Giant Green Anemone, named for its vibrant green tentacles and body. The green color is largely the result of microscopic-sized algae which live in the

tissues of the anemone, producing a green pigment due to photosynthesis. This relationship between the algae and the anemone is called "mutualism" because they both benefit from the association. The algae produce oxygen and organic compounds used by the anemone and the anemone produces carbon dioxide used by the algae. Anemones which live in shaded areas have little or no algae in their tissues and are paler green or even white. Although this anemone can reach a size of up to 10 inches, it is more commonly 4-6 inches across, and is found in the high to low intertidal zones in areas where there is plenty of wave activity.

Plate 13. AGGREGATING ANEMONE (*Anthopleura elegantissima*)
This anemone is found carpeting many of the rocks in the tidepools. Although it can reproduce sexually by releasing eggs and sperm into the water, it commonly reproduces asexually by cloning in which it produces an exact replica of itself by splitting in half. This process takes place fairly quickly (about 2-3 days) and may be a response to starving since two small anemones have twice the mouth surface-to-volume ratio as does a single large anemone. During periods of low tide, masses of Aggregating Anemone cover their tentacles with small bits of shell material and retract within themselves to keep from drying out (see Plate 13). As soon as high tide returns, they open their tentacles, dropping any attached shells, and begin feeding again.

WORMS

[*There are hundreds of species of marine worms, most looking quite different from worms you may be familiar with on land. Many species of marine worms have a ring of feathery "tentacles" called a plume surrounding the mouth and which the worm can retract into its tube when disturbed or exposed to air. Although worms are extremely abundant in tidepools, they are usually not seen because most of them live in tubes or burrow into the sand.*]

Plates 14a&b. SAND CASTLE WORM (*Phragmatopoma californica*)
The name of this worm is derived from the nature of the worm's tube, which it constructs by gluing together sand grains with a mucous secretion. Hundreds of adjacent worm tubes packed together form a massive honey-combed structure. These sandy masses occur on the sides of rocks in the middle to low intertidal zones in places where there is enough sand for the worms to construct their tubes. Care should be taken not to step on the delicate structures for they are easily crushed. The worm itself has a short black plume and retracts into the tube so that it is rarely seen.

MOLLUSCS

[*Molluscs are the largest group of invertebrates represented in tide-pools. All molluscs have a fleshy, muscular appendage called a "foot" which is modified for certain functions depending on the type of organism. For example, in many clams this foot is shovel-shaped and used for burrowing into the sediment. In snails and limpets, the foot is used to creep along slowly or to attach firmly to rocks. The shells of molluscs are highly treasured by beachcombers and collectors for their great variety of shape, color and ornamentation. Many shells, especially of the abalones, have a thick, inner pearly layer of iridescent shell material (sometimes called "mother of pearl") used for jewelry and inlay. This layer is generally hidden beneath an outer layer which has a rougher, duller appearance. The most common molluscs found in tidepools can be subdivided into three smaller groups (clams, snails and chitons) discussed separately below.*]

MUSSELS AND OTHER CLAMS

Mussels and clams have two shells which, in most cases, match each other. Although many clams burrow into the sand, those usually found in tidepools attach to rocks. Mussels are by far the most common example of this. They attach to the rocks with strong fibers called "byssal threads," what chefs commonly call the "beard" and cut away before cooking. The mussel can voluntarily dissolve these threads and gradually move to another part of the rock when they become over-crowded. Other clams found in rocky areas cement one of their shells to the rocks. In these clams, the two shells look much different from each other, the attaching shell being quite a bit larger and more cup-shaped. The Jewel Box Clam is a good example and is common in Southern California's tidepools.

NOTE: Although mussels and other clams provide a tasty meal, caution should be used in gathering them, for they can be highly poisonous during certain times of year. Many clams, especially mussels, feed on microscopic plankton suspended in the water. During summer and fall months, a particular species of toxic plankton called *Gonyaulax catenella* is more abundant in the waters off Southern California. The toxins of this plankton become concentrated in the tissues of mussels and can be lethal to humans who eat them. As a rule, you should eat mussels (and other clams) harvested only during the months of November through April.

Plate 15. CALIFORNIA MUSSEL (*Mytilus californianus*)
The elongate shells of the California Mussel have a brownish-black

outer layer which may be worn thin in places to reveal an inner layer of iridescent purple. The shells are generally 3-4 inches long but may reach 7 inches or more. California Mussels occur in thick, tightly packed clusters in the high to low intertidal zones and are usually associated with leaf barnacles. The tight packing of the mussels makes them more difficult for the starfish to prey upon since the starfish cannot get a strong grip on the two valves of a single mussel to pry open. Mussels make an excellent meal but, as mentioned above, caution should be used to avoid eating them during certain times of the year.

Plate 16. JEWEL BOX CLAM *(Chama arcana)*
This clam attaches by cementing one of its shells to a rock in the middle to low intertidal zone. The attaching shell is deeply convex and is covered by a small, flat upper shell (resulting in its name). It is shiny white with shades of pink and lavender intermixed.

SNAILS, ABALONES, AND LIMPETS

Members of this large group of molluscs have a broad, muscular "foot" used for creeping slowly over rocks and other surfaces. The foot of the abalone is highly prized for its sweet and delicious flavor. Buried within the foot of many species is a feeding structure called a "radula." The radula usually has rows of many small teeth used for grinding plant material from rocks or for drilling holes into the shells of other molluscs to devour the organism inside. Evidence of this drilling is commonly seen in clam shells and other snails which have a perfectly circular hole piercing the shell. Most members of this group have a single coiled shell, and are commonly called "snails." Other members have a shell in which the coiling is not obvious because the last "whorl" (or coil) of the shell is large, giving the shell a dish-shaped appearance. Examples are the abalone and limpet. Some species such as the Scaly Tube Snail have an irregularly sinuous and worm-like shell. In soft-bodied snails, an outer shell is completely absent, having been increasingly reduced through evolution until no shell is produced. The sea hare and nudibranch are good examples, and although they don't have a protective shell, they have different adaptations to perpetuate the species. One of these adaptations was mentioned previously—the sea hare lays eggs so prolifically (up to 100 million per month) that many will usually survive. The nudibranch, on the other hand, is frequently toxic to predators and therefore is generally avoided as prey.

Plate 17. BLACK TEGULA *(Tegula funebralis)*
Probably the most common snail in Southern California's tidepools is the Black Tegula. The outer layer of its shell is black to purple and may

be worn in places to reveal an inner, pearly layer. This snail feeds on algae in the middle to high intertidal zones. The shell is typically 1 to 1½ inches across. Empty Black Tegula shells are commonly used by hermit crabs as a mobile shelter.

Plate 18. WAVY TURBAN *(Astraea undosa)*
Spiralling down the length of this snail is a ridge with strong, wavy sculpturing giving it a knobby appearance in places. The tan outer layer of the shell covers an inner, pearly layer. The shell is two to four inches across and frequently has a tuft of Coralline Red Algae attached. This snail is common in the low intertidal zone and in kelp beds where it grazes on seaweed.

Plate 19. GRAY PERIWINKLE *(Littorina planaxis)*
This tiny snail is actually better adapted to air exposure than to extended submersion, and is more common in the spray zone than in the intertidal zones. It has a dull gray shell from one half to nearly an inch long. It is common to see a dozen or so Gray Periwinkles clustered together in a protected rock depression where they graze on algae and actually rasp away the surface of the rock as well.

Plate 20. EMARGINATE DOGWINKLE *(Nucella emarginata)*
Dogwinkles are similar to Periwinkles but are broader because their last whorl is inflated. The shell is about an inch or two in length with colors of yellow, tan and dark brown. Spiral ribs extending the length of the shell may be variously colored, giving it a banded appearance. Emarginate Dogwinkles are carnivorous, drilling a circular borehole into the shells and plates of mussels, limpets and barnacles. They are found associated with mussel beds in the high to middle intertidal zones.

Plate 21. PURPLE OLIVE *(Olivella biplicata)*
The highly polished shell of this snail is buff to medium brown, often with shades of lavender. The shell can reach a length of an 1½ inches but is usually less than an inch. The Purple Olive is fairly common in the middle to low intertidal zones, especially in sandier tidepools.

Plate 22. CHESTNUT COWRY *(Cypraea spadicea)*
This beautiful snail is found in the low intertidal zone and in pools in higher intertidal zones as well. It has a shiny shell with a chestnut-colored area on its upper surface bordered by a dark band. The fleshy "mantle" partially covering the shell is often bright orange and covered with small dark spots. The Chestnut Cowry is about 1 to 2½ inches long and is the only cowry in waters off California.

Plate 23. SCALY TUBE SNAIL *(Serpulorbis squamigerus)*
The unusual shell of this snail is twisted and sinuous, resembling a

worm tube more than a snail shell. Massive clusters of Scaly Tube Snails are often found attached to rocks. Individual tubes are about ¼ to ½ inch across, and may be several inches long. The tubes are chalky white to pale buff or gray with glossy white interiors. Broad longitudinal ribs and fine transverse growth lines give it a scaly appearance. The snail retracts into its worm-like shell during low tide and only its foot can be seen as a dark circle within the tube. Scaly Tube Snails are found under rock overhangs and on the sides of rocks in the middle to low intertidal zone.

ABALONES

The abalone is prized not only for its tasty meat but also for its beautiful shell. When the rough, dull outer layer is removed, an inner layer of iridescent shell is exposed. The iridesence may be purplish black, red, green or white, depending on the type of abalone. The shell has several holes aligned in a curve which are increasingly larger near the shell's edge. Each of these holes was once an opening for a tube through which the abalone's waste and respired water were expelled. As the abalone grows, more shell material forms around a new, larger hole. All abalones are grazers, feeding on seaweed and kelp beds. Their two long antennae and numerous "feelers" extend as a fringe around the edge of the shell. Three different species live in Southern California's waters, and black abalone is the most common. Unfortunately, all abalones are now rarely seen due to careless collecting.

Plate 24. BLACK ABALONE (*Haliotis cracherodii*)
The Black Abalone is generally 2-6 inches long with a fairly smooth shell. The outer surface of the Black Abalone is bluish- to greenish-black with fine growth lines running parallel to the shell's margin and 5 to 8 open respiratory holes. The inner surface is pearly white with faint green to pink iridescence. The flesh of the Black Abalone is inferior to that of other abalones, making it of little commercial value.

LIMPETS

The limpet is characterized by a single cap-shaped shell. The "keyhole" limpet derives its name from the single long opening at the top of the shell through which a fleshy tube expels waste products and respired water. Examples of keyhole limpets in Southern California's tidepools are the Giant Keyhole Limpet and the Volcano Limpet. The "true" limpet (all other limpets described below) lacks any opening in the top of its shell.

Plate 25. GIANT KEYHOLE LIMPET *(Megathura crenulata)*
The oval shell of this large limpet is gray to pale pink or yellow and has a large oval hole in the center. Radiating from this hole are a number of fine ridges. The shell is seldom seen in live specimens since the large fleshy "mantle" of the Giant Keyhole Limpet completely covers the shell. Although this mantle can be retracted somewhat, revealing a central portion of the shell, it cannot be completely retracted. The color of the mantle varies from a mottled tan or gray to black. The Giant Keyhole Limpet is commonly over 4 inches long and feeds on seaweeds in the low intertidal zone.

Plate 26. VOLCANO LIMPET *(Fissurella volcano)*
The shell of this small keyhole limpet may be pink, purple, gray or rust with darker bands radiating from its long, central hole. Unlike the Giant Keyhole Limpet, the shell of the Volcano Limpet is always visible. Its average length is ½-1 inch. It is common in the middle and low intertidal zones where it grazes on algal coatings under rocks.

Plate 27. ROUGH LIMPET *(Collisella scabra)*
This inch-long limpet has many strong ribs radiating from the top of the shell to its margins, producing scalloped edges. Its color may be tan, gray or light olive with ribs that are white to buff. The Rough Limpet prefers the high intertidal and spray zones.

Plate 28. FILE LIMPET *(Collisella limatula)*
The shell of the File Limpet is brown to green, often with shades of yellow. Fine ribs radiating from the top of the shell give this limpet a file-like appearance. It is 1-1½ inches long and is common in the high to middle intertidal zone.

Plate 29. GIANT OWL LIMPET *(Lottia gigantea)*
The low broad shell of the Giant Owl Limpet may be up to 4 inches long, making it the largest true limpet in North America. Its color is tan to dark brown with long white patches occurring as radiating bands usually near the margin. The top of the shell may be worn revealing a pearly inner layer. The Giant Owl Limpet requires vigorous wave activity and is found in the high and middle intertidal zones.

SOFT-BODIED SNAILS

These "snails" do not have an outer shell, so their soft tissues are exposed. However, they are equipped with other adaptations allowing them to escape predation. For example, sea hares are well camouflaged among algae and cobbles and, along with sea slugs, are able to discharge a cloud of ink to confuse the predator. A nudibranch (pronounced "nude-i-brank") is a soft-bodied snail in which the gills are exposed on its upper surface (the name "nudibranch" means "naked gills") as tufts or short tentacles. Although many nudibranchs are exquisitely colored, they are often poisonous and are avoided by predators. Others feed on certain organisms having the same coloration, thus camouflaging the nudibranch. To further guarantee survival, all of these soft-bodied snails are "hermaphroditic": each individual may function as both male and female. Because of this, they are highly prolific (producing up to 100 million eggs per month), thus ensuring a continuation of the species in spite of their lack of protective "armor."

Plate 30a&b. CALIFORNIA SEA HARE *(Aplysia californica)*

The California Sea Hare averages 6-8 inches in length and has two thin flaps of tissue which meet along the middle of its back, giving it a ruffled appearance. The sea hare undulates these flaps to move. It derives its name from the two long appendages which occur on the back of its head, making it appear rabbit-like. It has an irregular, mottled color with patches and streaks of rust, gray, green and black derived from the pigments of the algae it eats. This mottled coloring provides the animal with an effective camouflage among algae. It is also well camouflaged among cobbles, where it is often found. The worm-like egg masses are pink to pale yellow (see Plate 30b). When disturbed, the California Sea Hare discharges a cloud of purple ink which serves as a "smoke screen" allowing it to escape its predators. They can be found in protected pools in the middle and low intertidal zones.

Plate 31. STRIPED SEA SLUG *(Navanax inermis)*

The body of this colorful snail is typically 2-4 inches long and ¼-½ inch wide, although they can be double that size. They look almost velvety with a background color of dark brown or black with thin stripes and small specks of yellow, orange, white and bright, almost iridescent blue. The two wing-like flaps meeting along the middle of its back are edged in orange or yellow. The head has a pair of short, broad antennae, and the tail splits into two pointed extensions. It lays stringy egg masses and ejects a yellow ink when disturbed. The Striped Sea Slug is carnivorous; in tidepools it feeds mostly on bubble snails, nudibranchs and sea hares.

Plate 32. SPANISH SHAWL NUDIBRANCH
(Flabellinopsis iodinea)

This vivid nudibranch has a purple body with orange projections and a pair of bright red gill tufts. It is typically an inch or two long and lives in the middle to low intertidal zones where it feeds on small hydroid corals. It can swim by quickly flexing its body in U-shaped bends.

Plate 33. HOPKINS' ROSE *(Hopkinsia rosacea)*
Appropriately named, the Hopkins' Rose is a vivid rosy pink with long, pink fingerlike projections covering its back. Its coloration is the same as that of the pink bryozoan on which it feeds, thus camouflaging this brightly-colored nudibranch. Its ribbon-like egg masses are also vivid pink. Hopkins' Rose can be found in protected pools and under rocks in the low intertidal zone. It is small, usually only ¼-½ inch long.

CHITONS

A chiton (pronounced "kite-un") is characterized by eight plates surrounded by an oval-shaped "girdle" and a fleshy foot used to attach to rocks. Embedded in this foot is a radula used to scrape algae and other plant material from the surface of rocks. Some chitons are quite mobile, creeping over the rocks in search of food. Others, such as the Troglodyte Chiton, are more sedentary, remaining in a single depression of rock throughout their lives.

Plates 34a&b. TROGLODYTE CHITON *(Nuttalina fluxa)*
Although several species of chitons inhabit Southern California's tidepools, one of the most common and interesting ones is the Troglodyte Chiton. This brown to green creature is 1-2 inches long with a mossy-looking girdle patched with short white spines. The Troglodyte Chiton scrapes a depression in the rock as it feeds on microscopic plant material settling into this ever-deepening hole. This depression also protects the chiton from heavy surf and predators. Several generations of chitons may occupy a specific depression. The Troglodyte Chiton is especially common in soft rocks such as those around Laguna and La Jolla where thousands of oval-shaped depressions mark their presence *(see Plate 34b).*

Plate 35. CONSPICUOUS CHITON *(Stenoplax conspicua)*
This large chiton (up to 4 inches long) is generally found in sandy areas of the tidepool under stones to avoid sunlight. It can crawl fairly quickly and emerges at night to feed. The plates are light green to gray and may be white or pink in worn areas. The girdle is leathery and covered with tiny scales. It is found in the middle to low intertidal zone.

Plate 1. Common Surfgrass. Puerco Beach, Los Angeles Co.

Plate 2. Spongeweed. Dike Rock, San Diego Co.

Plate 3. Sea Lettuce. Big Rock Point, San Diego Co.

Plate 4. Sea Bubble. Whale View Point, San Diego Co.

Plate 5. Sargasso Weed. Big Rock Point, San Diego Co.

Plate 6. Rockweed. Big Rock Point, San Diego Co.

Plate 7. Southern Sea Palm. North Bird Rock, San Diego Co.

Plate 8. Feather Boa Kelp showing fine and flat blades. Dike Rock, San Diego Co.

Plate 9. Coralline Red Algae. Alligator Head, San Diego Co.

Plate 10. Pink Encrusting Coralline Algae. Whale View Point, San Diego Co.

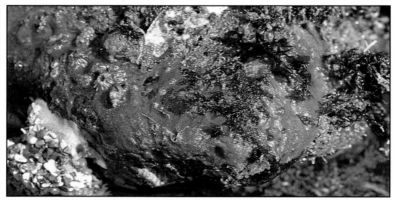

Plate 11. Velvety Red Sponge. Dike Rock, San Diego Co.

Plate 12. A colorful Giant Green Anemone. Puerco Beach, Los Angeles Co.

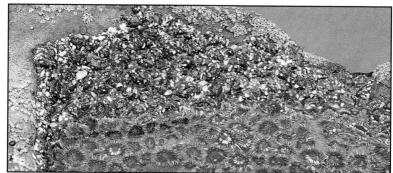

Plate 13. Aggregating Anemones. Those under water have their tentacles open for feeding while those that are exposed above the water line are closed. Attached shell particles help keep those anemones from drying out. Dike Rock, San Diego Co.

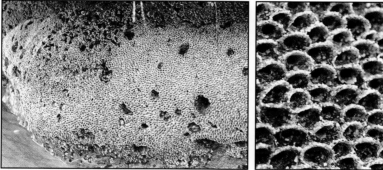

Plate 14. (a) A large mass of Sand Castle Worm tubes. Striped Shore Crabs often inhabit the larger holes. (b) Close up of Sand Castle Worm tubes. Note that they are made up of sand grains. Sea Cliff Co. Park, San Diego Co.

Plate 15. California Mussels. Dike Rock, San Diego Co.

Plate 16. Jewel Box Clam. Dike Rock, San Diego Co.

Plate 17. Black Tegulas. Big Rock Point, San Diego Co.

Plate 18. Wavy Turban with its large fleshy "foot" extended. Note the algae attached to the shell, effectively camouflaging this snail. Bird Rock, San Diego Co.

Plate 19. Gray Periwinkles. Big Rock Point, San Diego Co.

Plate 20. Emarginate Dogwinkles feeding on a cluster of Leaf Barnacles. False Point, San Diego Co.

Plate 21. Purple Olives. Dike Rock, San Diego Co.

Plate 22. Chestnut Cowry showing a portion of its spotted mantle. White Point, Los Angeles Co.

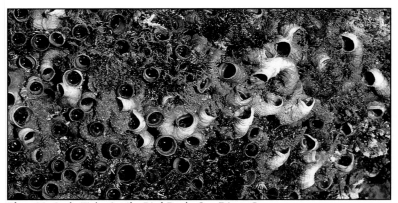

Plate 23. Scaly Tube Snails. Bird Rock, San Diego Co.

Plate 24. Black Abalone. Puerco Beach, Los Angeles Co.

Plate 25. Giant Keyhole Limpet. Note that the light colored fleshy mantle nearly covers the shell. False Point, San Diego Co.

Plate 26. Volcano Limpets. Dike Rock, San Diego Co.

Plate 27. Rough Limpets. Big Rock Point, San Diego Co.

Plate 28. File Limpet. La Jolla Cove, San Diego Co.

Plate 29. Giant Owl Limpet with other smaller limpets attached. Hospital Point, San Diego Co.

Plate 30. (a) California Sea Hares. Note that their coloration closely matches that of the surrounding algae. False Point, San Diego Co. (b) Egg mass of California Sea Hares washed up on the beach. Casa Cove, San Diego Co.

Plate 31. Striped Sea Slug. Bird Rock, San Diego Co.

Plate 32. Spanish Shawl Nudibranch. Its exposed gills are clearly seen as two bright red tufts just behind its tentacles. Torrey Pines State Beach, San Diego Co.

Plate 33. Hopkins' Rose Nudibranch. White Point, Los Angeles Co.

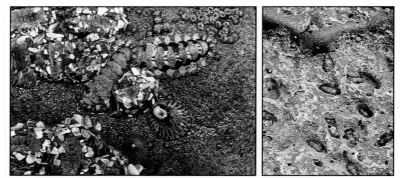

Plate 34. (a) Close-up of Troglodyte Chitons. Dike Rock, San Diego Co. (b) Troglodyte Chitons in oval-shaped depressions in a soft sandstone. Big Rock Point, San Diego Co.

Plate 35. Conspicuous Chitons. Bird Rock, San Diego Co.

Plate 36. Blue-Legged Hermit Crab in a tegula shell. Dike Rock, San Diego Co.

Plate 37. Striped Shore Crab. North Bird Rock, San Diego Co.

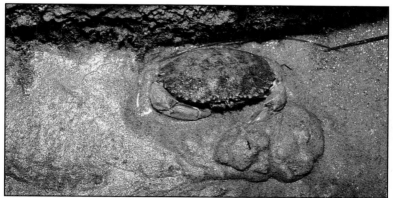

Plate 38. Rock Crab burrowing in the sand. Dike Rock, San Diego Co.

Plate 39. California Spiny Lobsters. Scripps Aquarium-Museum, San Diego Co.

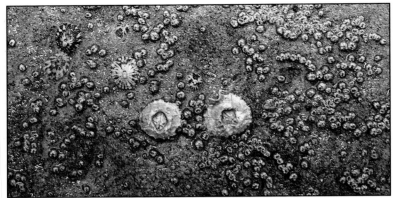

Plate 40. Acorn Barnacles. Dike Rock, San Diego Co.

Plate 41. Volcano Barnacles. Whale View Point, San Diego Co.

Plate 42. Leaf Barnacles (a) exposed to air and (b) with feathery "feet" extended for feeding. Point Loma, San Diego Co.

Plate 43. Purple Sea Urchins surrounding a single Red Sea Urchin. White Point, Los Angeles Co.

Plate 44. Warty Sea Cucumber. Bird Rock, San Diego Co.

Plate 45. Bat Star. Bird Rock, San Diego Co.

Plate 46. Ochre Sea Stars. White Point, Los Angeles Co.

Plate 47. Panama Brittle Star. Dike Rock, San Diego Co.

Plate 48. Stalked Tunicates. Mussel Shoals, Ventura Co.

CRABS, LOBSTERS, BARNACLES

[*Members of this large group all have jointed legs and antennae. It may seem surprising that the barnacle also belongs to this group. Its outer shell has been modified into sturdy, overlapping plates, but like other members, the barnacle inside has jointed legs and antennae.*]

Plate 36. BLUE-LEGGED HERMIT CRAB (*Pagurus samuelis*)
The teardrop-shaped body of this crab is seldom seen. It lives within the empty shell of a snail, usually that of the Black Tegula. Its olive-colored body is propelled by long, thin legs tipped with bright blue bands. As the hermit crab grows, it discards the shell it is living in for a larger one. The Blue-Legged Hermit Crab is abundant in the high and middle intertidal zones, particularly where cobbles and pebbles abound (e.g. La Jolla Cove and False Point). This scavenger feeds on plant material and dead organisms. The Blue-Legged Hermit Crab does not do well out of water for extended periods of time.

Plate 37. STRIPED SHORE CRAB (*Pachygrapsus crassipes*)
One of the most common crabs in the high and middle intertidal zones is the Striped Shore Crab. The background color of its body is dark green, brownish or purple marked by transverse stripes of paler green or purple. The Striped Shore Crab can live in both air and water, and eats a wide range of food including plant material, dead organisms, live molluscs and hermit crabs. During the day, it frequently hides in crevices and under rocks.

Plate 38. ROCK CRAB (*Cancer antennarius*)
The sturdy Rock Crab has strong pincers and short walking legs which it uses to burrow into the sand near rocks, making it difficult to find on sunny days. Its shell is lavender to reddish purple on top and cream-colored underneath; its pincers are black-tipped. The Rock Crab's oval-shaped body is usually 2-4 inches across. It lives from the high to low intertidal zones where it is both a scavenger and a carnivore. One of its favorite meals is the hermit crab for which it uses its powerful pincers to break the hermit crab's protective shell.

Plate 39. CALIFORNIA SPINY LOBSTER (*Panulirus interruptus*)
This bright reddish-brown lobster is generally 8-12 inches long, but can attain lengths of over 2 feet. The California Spiny Lobster has spines extending down from the sides of its outer shell and a pair protruding above its eyes. It has no claws. Although commercially important for its meat, it lacks the flavor and tenderness of other cold-water lobsters.

BARNACLES

Barnacles all have numerous limy plates, which they can open up to feed, or close to protect themselves from drying out. Those exposed during low tides are closed, so that all that is visible are their plates. If you visit a tidepool during middle to high tide, you might be able to see barnacles on wave-swept rocks with their long, feathery "feet" protruding from between their open plates as they devour microscopic plankton (see Plate 42b). Barnacles live attached to rocks and other solid objects such as shells, buoys, boats and even whales. Some of the breaching (jumping) behavior of whales is believed to be an attempt by the whale to dislodge irritating barnacles from its body.

Basically, two types of barnacles live in Southern California's tidepools. The most common and abundant barnacles are cap-shaped with a wide base attached firmly to the rocks. Their outermost plates are fused and only their inner plates are movable. Examples are the acorn and volcano barnacles (see Plates 40 & 41). Their attachment is so strong that acorn barnacles can grip vertical rock faces where other organisms are washed away. The other type of barnacle has a thin, fleshy stalk terminating in several flattened plates giving this barnacle a leaf-like appearance. This is the leaf barnacle (see Plates 42a&b), sometimes called the goosenecked barnacle because of the shape of its stalk.

Plate 40. ACORN BARNACLE *(Chthamalus spp. and Balanus spp.)*
Several species are commonly referred to as "Acorn" barnacles. The different species can be distinguished by the arrangement of their plates. The Acorn Barnacle ranges from about ½ to 1 inch across and may be whitish (most common) to tan or brown. It is cap-shaped and its individual plates are clearly obvious. It is commonly preyed upon by the Emarginate Dogwinkle and the Ochre Sea Star. The Acorn Barnacle is common in the high to middle intertidal zone.

Plate 41. VOLCANO BARNACLE *(Tetraclita rubescens)*
This colorful barnacle is common in the high to low intertidal zone. Its color ranges from pink to brown and is about 1 to 2 inches across. It has a high profile on the rocks and its inner movable plates are usually recessed and difficult to see. The outer fused plates are essentially indistinguishable from each other and have deep, parallel grooves.

Plates 42a&b. LEAF BARNACLE *(Pollicipes polymerus)*
This stalked barnacle is characterized by 6 large white plates and several additional small plates, all of which are white to gray. The stalk is dark gray to dark brown and has numerous scaly or spiny protrusions. Many individual Leaf Barnacles form massive, circular clumps

commonly associated with the California Mussel in the high intertidal zone. These clumps make the Leaf Barnacle less susceptible to predation by the Ochre Sea Star. They also live in the middle and low intertidal zones. Leaf Barnacles exposed during low tide are retracted (to prevent drying out) causing their stalks to appear short and wide.

STARFISH, SEA URCHINS, SEA CUCUMBERS

[*Most members of this group have spines embedded in their skin. These spines are conspicuous in sea urchins, but are less obvious in sand dollars and many starfish whose fuzzy appearance is due to the tiny spines protruding from their bodies. Many members also have what is called "pentameral" or five-part symmetry, as is obvious in sea stars and brittle stars, but is also true of sea urchins. One of the most interesting characteristics of this group, however, is the ability to regenerate lost body parts. Many years ago before this became common knowledge, oyster fishermen would cut up starfish that were preying on their oysters and throw the pieces back into the sea. To their misfortune, many of these "pieces" grew into complete starfish, thus increasing many-fold the starfish population in the oyster beds. This regenerative ability has limits; a portion of the central area of the starfish is needed for regeneration to occur. In some species of brittle stars the entire central region must be present. The regeneration is slow, taking up to a year to complete. An interesting adaptation of this regeneration is exhibited by the sea cucumber which can expel its internal organs and then grow new replacements. This is done on a yearly basis by many sea cucumbers but may also be done in response to predation. A predator, which would normally eat the entire sea cucumber, is instead "offered" a substitute meal of the sea cucumber's organs, thus satisfying the predator and allowing the sea cucumber to escape.*

Most members possess bulb-like "tube feet." In the starfish, these feet line the grooves on the underside of each arm and can extend and retract. They function as sensory organs in brittle stars and for locomotion in sea stars. Sea stars and sea urchins also have little "suction cups" on the tips of their tube feet which allow them to attach firmly to rocks and other objects. Sea stars use these suction cups to grasp the two shells of a mussel or other clam and pry them apart so that they can devour the tender animal inside.

Although sand dollars and heart urchins are also members of this group, they are not included in this book because they inhabit sandy beaches and not the rocky intertidal.]

Plate 43. PURPLE SEA URCHIN *(Strongylocentrotus purpuratus)*
This lovely sea urchin is 2-4 inches across and covered with ½-1 inch spines. The adults are vivid purple (almost reddish on the body) whereas the juveniles are greenish. These urchins scrape rock surfaces for algae and wear crevices into these rocks. Commonly, they are found living in these self-made homes. The Purple Sea Urchin is common in the low intertidal zone in wave-swept areas, but may be washed by strong surf into higher parts of the tidepool.

Plate 43. RED SEA URCHIN *(Strongylocentrotus franciscanus)*
The Red Sea Urchin may be up to 5 inches across with spines 2-3 inches long. It lives in the low intertidal zone and in kelp beds where it grazes on kelp. Although overpopulation of the Red Sea Urchin nearly destroyed California's kelp beds many years ago, their numbers have been brought under control, in part by the re-introduction of the California Sea Otter, one of its main predators. The Red Sea Urchin is not as common in the intertidal as the Purple Sea Urchin.

Plate 44. WARTY SEA CUCUMBER *(Parastichopus parvimensis)*
The common name of this organism is derived from its cucumber shape and the numerous warty projections covering its body. It is generally 6-10 inches long and is red to dark brown, with short, black-tipped projections. The Warty Sea Cucumber lives in the low intertidal zone where it feeds on organic material in the sediment.

SEA STARS

Members of this group of starfish have 5 stout arms equipped with numerous tube feet and suction cups for locomotion and feeding. Their central body region is not readily distinguished from the arms.

Plate 45. BAT STAR *(Patiria miniata)*
Five short, triangular-shaped arms extend from the body of this sea star, giving it a distinctively star-shaped appearance. It is usually bright orange, but may be a variety of other colors, as well as highly mottled, and has a fairly smooth surface lacking spines. Bat Stars prefer the low intertidal to subtidal zones where they feed on seaweed, molluscs and sponges.

Plate 46. OCHRE SEA STAR *(Pisaster ochraceus)*
The five radiating arms of this sea star are thick and longer than those of the Bat Star. It is rough and covered with many short white spines. The Ochre Sea Star is orange to red or brown and may reach a diameter of 20 inches, although it is more commonly 4-8 inches across. It lives in the middle to low intertidal zones and feeds primarily on molluscs—especially the California Mussel. It also feeds on limpets, chitons and barnacles.

BRITTLE STARS

They look quite different from sea stars, having a distinct central body region, called a "central disk," and five long, thin arms, giving it a spidery appearance. They usually hide under rocks by day and come out at night to feed. Their tube feet function mainly as sensory organs. When disturbed, a brittle star easily loses one or more arms (which it will eventually regenerate), resulting in the name "brittle star."

Plate 47. PANAMA BRITTLE STAR *(Ophioderma panamense)*
The pentagonal central disk of the Panama Brittle Star is 1-1½ inch across and mottled olive to brown color. The 6-8 inch arms are the same color as the central disk but also have buff or gray bands. Rows of short spines run along the sides of the arms. This brittle star dwells under rocks in the middle and low intertidal zones where it searches for food with its tube feet. When it finds something edible, it coils one of its long arms around it to draw the snack to its centrally-located mouth.

TUNICATES

[Tunicates are very different from other animals described in this chapter. They are primitive "chordates," a large group including vertebrates such as fish and humans. Chordates are characterized by having all of the following during some phase of their life: (1) a notochord (a flexible supportive rod running the length of the body); (2) pharyngeal gill slits; (3) a hollow dorsal nerve cord. Like most of the other tidepool animals, larval tunicates are mobile, swimming through the water until they settle on a substrate and undergo metamorphosis to become an adult. During this metamorphosis, the notochord and most of the dorsal nerve cord are lost. The name "tunicate" is derived from the leathery "tunic" covering the body.]

Plate 48. STALKED TUNICATE *(Styela montereyensis)*
This tunicate attaches to rocks in the low intertidal zone. It has a slender stalk with a body that may be yellow, reddish brown or orange. Although they may grow quite large (up to 10 inches long), they are usually much smaller. Those I observed were about 3-5 inches long. Stalked tunicates look much like wilted flower buds when exposed during low tide.

Appendix

~~~~~~~~~~~~~~~~~~~

Tides are the periodic rise and fall of the sea resulting from the gravitational attraction between the earth, moon and sun. This attraction literally pulls the earth's water toward the moon and sun. The amount of pull between two bodies depends on their mass and the distance between them. The greater the mass of a body, the greater its attraction to another. And the closer the two bodies are, the greater their gravitational pull will be. Thus, the sun has a strong effect on the earth's tides because of its enormous mass, while the moon's importance comes from its proximity to earth. Despite its relatively low mass, the moon has a greater effect on our tides than the sun because of its nearness. Thus we find that the earth's tides are affected primarily by the moon's rotation around the earth and secondarily by the earth's rotation relative to the sun. Because the moon has the greatest effect on the earth's tides, let's consider it first.

The earth makes a complete rotation relative to the moon every 24 hours and 50 minutes. As the earth rotates, the portion of the oceans closest to the moon bulges moonward because of the moon's gravitational pull (see Figure 2a). The ocean on the opposite side of the earth also bulges, but away from the moon (although not as much) due to centrifugal force (which pulls the water away from the earth's surface) and because the gravitational attraction on this side of the earth is not as great (being farther from the moon). As the earth rotates relative to the moon, the two tidal bulges result in higher water levels or "high tides." On the sides of the earth between these bulges, the water level is lower, producing "low tides." If the moon were all we had to consider, the high and low tides would always be nearly the same height. Now let's consider the effects of the sun on the earth's tides.

When the sun is in a straight line with the moon relative to the earth (see Figure 2b), the gravitational pull on the oceans is at its greatest because of the combined effects of the moon and the sun, and the resulting bulges, or high tides, are unusually high. On the sides of the earth perpendicular to these bulges, the water is at its lowest, and we experience very low tides. We call this a "spring tide" which occurs when the moon is full and when it is new (roughly every 14 days). As an example of typical tide levels in Southern California, we might have a high tide of 6.1 ft. and a low tide of -0.3 ft. We have the most extreme spring tides during the winter months, causing high tides to be very high and low tides to be very low. Therefore, it is best to visit tidepools during the spring tides of winter.

It takes approximately 28 days for the moon to rotate around the earth. During its first and third quarters, the moon is aligned at right angles to the sun (see Figure 2c), resulting in a gravitational pull that is more evenly distributed on the earth's oceans. We call this a "neap tide" and it is characterized by lower high tides and higher low tides. In Southern California, typical tide levels during this time might be a 4.5 ft. high tide and a 0.8 ft. low tide.

Since it takes 24 hrs. and 50 min. for the earth to make a complete rotation relative to the moon, it takes half that time (about 12 hrs. and 25 min.) for successive bulges to pass the same point on the earth's surface (in an idealized situation). Thus, in Southern California which has roughly two high and two low tides per day, we can expect that a high tide at 10:00 A.M. on Monday would be followed by another high tide twelve and a half hours later, about 10:30 P.M. Monday night. This is close to the times predicted in tide tables, but is slightly off due to other factors that also affect the movement of tidal "bulges" through our oceans. These factors include the bottom topography of the sea floor and coastal profiles. On certain rare days, Southern California has only one high and one low tide. As mentioned earlier, because the moon makes a complete rotation around the earth every 28 days, we experience a spring tide every 14 days (when the moon is full and again when it is new). This means that if the tides are low at noon on a Wednesday, the tides will be high at noon on the following Wednesday, and low again at noon the Wednesday after that, two weeks later. This is useful when timing your tidepool visits when you don't have a tide chart.

This knowledge will also help you to interpret and understand tide tables. Most of them indicate the phases of the moon and you will see how this corresponds to the tide levels during those times. It is best to visit tidepools when the tides are at their lowest. Obviously, the lowest low tides will occur when the moon is full and when it is new (particularly during the winter months), but any time the tide is low is satisfactory for tidepooling.

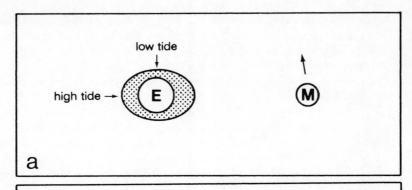

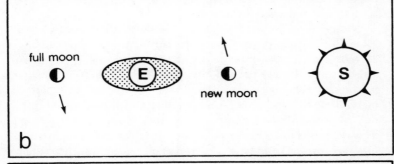

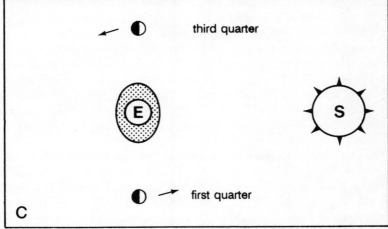

Figure 2. Relationship of earth (E) with the moon (M) and sun (S) to produce high and low tides. (a) High and low tides resulting from the moon's gravitational pull on earth. (b) Very high high tides and very low low tides result when the sun is aligned in a straight line with the moon relative to earth. (c) When the sun and moon are at right angles to each other relative to earth, the tidal fluctuations are modified to produce lower high tides and higher low tides. See text in the Appendix for a complete explanation.

Additional Reading

Many other books provide information about our coastal environment. The following are highly recommended.

Brandon, J.L. and F.J. Rokop, 1985. "Life Between the Tides." American Southwest Publ. Co., 228 pp.

California Coastal Commission, 1987. "California Coastal Resource Guide." University of California Press, 384 pp.

Fitch, J.E. and R.J. Lavenberg, 1975. "Tidepool and Nearshore Fishes of California." University of California Press, 156 pp.

Gotshall, D.W. and L.L. Laurent, 1979. "Pacific Coast Subtidal Marine Invertebrates." Sea Challengers, 107 pp.

Hinton, S., 1987. "Seashore Life of Southern California." University of California Press, 217 pp.

McConnaughey, B.H. and E. McConnaughey, 1986. "Pacific Coast (An Audubon Society Nature Guide)." Alfred A. Knopf, 633 pp.

Morris, R.H., D.P. Abbott, and E.C. Haderlie, 1980. "Intertidal Invertebrates of California." Stanford University Press, 690 pp.

Ricketts, E.F. and J. Calvin, 1968. "Between Pacific Tides. 4th Ed." Revised by J.W. Hedgepeth. Stanford University Press, 614 pp.

Sharp, R.P., 1978. "Coastal Southern California (A Kendall/Hunt Geology Field Guide Series)." Kendall/Hunt Publishing Co., 268 pp.

Wertheim, A., 1984. "The Intertidal Wilderness." Sierra Club Books, 156 pp.

Index

Index

Index

ABOUT THE AUTHOR

Linda Tway has been affiliated with Scripps Institution of Oceanography since 1982 when she began post-doctoral research there. She has had an intense interest in tidepools since she was an undergraduate studying the relationships of marine invertebrates and the rocks to which they attach. She has taught numerous classes in oceanography, geology and paleontology at several universities.